Contents

Listening

Prologue

What do you hear when you can't see a thing? How do you listen when you don't know who stands next to you? And then what do you say?

An attendant dressed in black guides me by the arm into a pitch-dark room, every nook and cranny of which is covered in black cloth. My elbow is released, and for a moment it feels like I am floating in nothingness. I begin to wobble, as if I'm standing on a mile-high pillar, a sensation that takes me back to my childhood. Then I notice that there are other bodies in the room, their breath vibrating in the air, their presence almost tangible.

"Hello." A greeting; the most basic ethical act.

▶ ▷ ▶

We—the invisible collective of participants in artist duo Lundahl & Seitl's *Infinite Conversations*—softly discuss how the darkness affects us.[1] It feels like I'm just a voice, I say, like my body has become sound. The genie isn't out of the bottle; it has become the bottle itself. It sounds pompous; I shut up again.

I ended up here because I'm looking for listening experiences, and I'm looking for such experiences because I want to practice paying attention. Not the attention that is focused on information, production, or even connection, but rather attention as the philosopher and mystic Simone Weil described it: empty and open.

The darkness is a welcome contrast to the excess of moving, luminous, and intrusive images that surround us daily. So is the silence, how our voices emerge from it, clear and hesitant, as if trying themselves out for the first time. But even the dark soon turns normal. I fall back into old habits, annoyances, judgments.

For now, I am mostly a tense performer of attention, even though no one can see me. Like Weil's students who frown, hold their breath, and sit up straight when they must pay attention. If you ask them what they've heard, they don't have an answer. They've tightened their muscles. And because they've physically tired themselves, they think, "I have worked well!"[2]

▶ ▷ ▶

Listening is hip. It is considered the opposite of looking, or visual culture, as well as speaking, or the expression of opinions. It makes a promise to the unsung and underrecognized, leaving an impression of courtesy. At the same time, it's a demand from those who feel unheard. Politicians and other higher-ups love it. So do artists.

Since listening is a practice of attention, and attention has been hijacked by modern technology, listening is also presented as a solution to the problem of technology. Or rather, to the host of problems that digitalization has brought about: distraction, narcissism, polarization, and a hardening of public debate that spills over into the streets.

An example. A University of Oxford report calls for a revaluation of the virtue of listening in education, at a time when attention has become an economic commodity. It is a civic duty to be a good listener, the report states, to learn to understand others and "go against the tide of our polarization."[3] I wonder what is meant by such virtuous listening. What listening entails exactly is often left in the dark, also by the politicians promising to do it and the media accusing themselves of failing in it. What happens when you open your ears to the world around you? The Oxford report characterizes the virtue of listening as "greater focus on passivity, introversion, humility and quietude, and reduced focus on agency, leadership and self-determination."[4] Our networking age demands values such as sharing and collaboration.

The quote brings me to my feet. Really? Should we become passive again? Contrasting speaking as an active act to listening as an inactive one seems too simplistic. As if all listening were obedience. I'd rather believe that paying attention to someone or something requires being steadfast and outward-looking, in other words: autonomous.

▶ ▷ ▶

What does it mean to be a good listener? Why is it important? What do you actually do when you listen? These are questions that imply an ethics of listening. Ethics is about actions, about how you move in the world and interact with others. What are better and worse ways to do that, what standards can be applied? How to draw the line between can, will, and must?

Listening is a concrete, though often invisible, act that bridges the gap between the self and the outside world, particularly other people. A relationship is established by paying attention. You cannot listen well without being attentive, nor without being receptive. While steadfast and outward-looking, you must also be open to what comes to you, to that which is unknown and unpredictable.

In this book I approach listening as such an ethical relationship. Furthermore, technology mediates this relationship between the self and the outside world. This does not only create obstacles. For example, social media may make listening difficult, but it has also enabled more people than ever before to make themselves heard.

Ethics and relations, technology and mediation: within the space of those four rather abstract terms, listening surfaces as a daily practice of paying attention. Ultimately, the relationship between sender and receiver, speaker and hearer, will make a turn. After all, those who listen have something to give, and those who speak receive it. But that's for later.

▶ ▷ ▶

My search for an ethics of listening began with myself listening. In January 2021, during the ongoing pandemic, I challenged myself to note down one name or reference related to listening and its ethics every day. I asked for input on social media and in meetings online and offline. My notebook quickly filled up and grew into an archive of listening resources. Many of these sources ended up in this book. Without all those people who shared their knowledge, references, and associations with me, I wouldn't have been able to write it. From the beginning, listening openly and unbiasedly was an indispensable method.

I listened with the ears of a philosopher in search of the ethical potential of an underexposed sense. Wait, "underexposed" is a visual metaphor. Indeed, when you start paying attention to it, you quickly notice how dominant images are in our language, culture, and thinking. And in philosophy.

Throughout history, Western philosophy has placed the greatest value on the visible, that which can easily be measured and described. For example, in his article "The Nobility of Sight," the philosopher Hans Jonas explains the value of the visual. He connects sight to freedom.[5] With our eyes we can hold an object, distance ourselves from it, put it away and retrieve it. Actions that are difficult or impossible with hearing or touch. Sound imposes itself on us; it robs us of our freedom.

Another reason that listening receives little attention in philosophy is the emphasis put on speaking. Since the Enlightenment, expressing yourself, being heard and outspoken, have been important conditions for autonomy, citizenship, and empowerment. If listening plays a role in philosophy at all, it's primarily to gain knowledge and serve the will to truth, implies Jean-Luc Nancy in his work titled *Listening*.[6] Whereas the importance of listening, I found, rather has to do with *not-knowing*. After all, if you already know something, you no longer need to listen.

The very first source I wrote down in my notebook was an article by the sociologist Rolando Vázquez Melken. He writes, "The task of listening presents itself also as an ethical orientation, toward knowledge as *relationality*."[7] It is through listening that you discover that a neutral point of view to consider the world does not exist. As a listener, you are always positioned in a certain relation to what you hear. This is very literally the case with sound. Walking down the street, in nature, or in an office or school building, the surrounding sound changes with your movement. This is not a defect, but a given. We have a perspective. The relationship that listening establishes is therefore a reversal of the will to truth. It is a movement toward "the opening of reception," writes Vázquez Melken.[8]

Listening establishes a relationship of ethical significance that is mediated by technology. I develop this argument in four essays, each with its own theme. The first essay dives into the context of technology. The second considers speaking to other people and the wish for dialogue. In the third essay, I approach listening as a form of testimony, mainly related to following war reporting and other news. Finally, the fourth essay focuses on listening to nonverbal sounds, such as music and nature. If we are to pay attention to the meaningful, there is much to be learned from listening to the meaningless.

Art plays a major role in this book. Art could also be understood as a technology or technique—an exceptional one, at that. To explore how art mediates listening, each essay begins with a vignette that tunes into an artistic or aural mediation. These hopefully express how listening is simultaneously accessible, difficult, friendly, disconcerting, satisfying, dependent, and autonomous.

1 The Context of Technology

VIGNETTE: THE NEW LISTENING

"All day long we're stuck in our own heads," says a voice. "But what if you could crawl into someone else's head for just a moment?"[1]

We usually get to know someone's experiences and perceptions from the outside, like in conversation, an interview, or a social media feed. Perceiving someone's reality from the inside seems impossible. Or could technology make someone's inner experience palpable? The podcast *In the Head of* tries to do so. Each episode features someone with, for example, autism, tinnitus, or PTSD, who describes how they experience the world, against a backdrop of sounds that reproduce their inner auditory experience. Apparently, sound plays a huge part in our inner experience. The soundtrack is recorded in "8D."

What all those dimensions are, I don't know. However, listening is a multidimensional experience in itself. Sound encompasses you; you are in the middle of it. Turn to your side and what you hear changes. Get distracted for a moment and the sounds have disappeared. With earplugs, it's different. On the one hand, they seem to cut away a dimension. I am removed from my surroundings. When I turn around with my headphones on, nothing changes. The sound moves with me as if I have a surround sound system attached to my body. I am the sun around which a tonal cosmos revolves. Take off my crown, and I become an object in the way of sound waves again.

On the other hand, the extension of my ears that such headphones are, in the terminology of Marshall McLuhan, constitutes proximity by sending sound directly into my head.[2] It can be a physical, intimate sensation, especially if you are sensitive to certain sounds or soundscapes. As R. Murray Schafer says, "Hearing is a way of touching at a distance."[3]

The popularity of podcasts proves that such intimacy works. Yet the same listening technology is blamed for hindering proximity. Expensive noise-canceling gadgets allow everyone to retreat into their own bubble; no one really listens to one another anymore, it is said. In other words, "the new listening" apparently leads to both attentive intimacy and indifferent detachment.

▶ ▷ ▶

"The New Listening" is the title of an empirical study on podcasts issued by a Dutch media company.[4] What's new about it is that you no longer need a radio to tune into a channel or broadcast. Now, you can listen whenever and wherever you want. The behavior that comes with it is also new. Since the lockdowns caused by the COVID-19 pandemic and the rise of working from home, the morning and evening rush hour listening peaks have disappeared. The whole day has become a long succession of listening moments.

One of the goals of the study was to determine the advertising potential of podcasts. Listening behavior is easy to quantify. Data and statistics tell you how many times an episode was played and for how long. Podcast listeners turn out to be attentive listeners, thanks to headphones and the bubble they create. This makes them an ideal audience for advertisers and creators alike. And so, "the new listening" is increasingly embedded in the existing media landscape. Voilà, there's your market.

"New" can also refer to something else entirely. For instance, anyone can start a podcast, and you don't have to be a professional. While there are significant differences in quality, podcasting remains an extremely accessible and democratic medium. This also gives rise to new forms, genres, and ways of storytelling, such as "chatcasts," "braindumps," and multi-episode stories.[5] Rather than crawling into another person's head, though, listeners are often left standing in the doorway. Sometimes, you can feel like nothing more than an excuse for other people's ramblings. Is this really about listening, or rather about speaking?

As far as I'm concerned, new listening is at its most new when it helps you notice, with the help of technology, what's going on out there. Be it sounds from the big city, nature, experimental music, or the inner voice of a fellow human being. Not necessarily facts or information, but unfamiliar sounds and aural perspectives, that let you encounter something that you normally don't hear. Such productions, which take as their subject the very act of listening, are a kind of listening exercise. They let you practice your "sonic sensibility."[6]

We crawl into the head of the world, even though it remains strange that to do so, we must first shut ourselves off from it with a headset.

MAKING YOURSELF HEARD

Let me start with a declaration of love.

On the internet you're never alone. You're never bored. Even if you're alone and bored, there's something to do. And, my God, how often have I been bored alone.

Writers are introverts, after all. But the internet gave writers—like everyone else—the opportunity to make themselves heard without having to leave the house, to network without a party. The internet *was* the party. Except what mattered was not a talent for small talk or the right outfit but, as crazy as it sounds these days, content. Anyone could see or read what you were up to as long as you kept publishing, on your own website or profile page, or together in an online magazine or journal.

I was late to the party. I started my own blog in 2008, which was just before the explosion of mobile internet and of social media, but still far from early. The blog opened doors that had previously been closed to me. It was the most "powerful leveling mechanism in the recent history of publishing."[7]

That itself is history now. All optimism about the internet and social media has proven to be short-sighted if not dangerous. Yes, anyone can and does make themselves heard.

Not only introverted writers, but also warmongers and other hateful radicals.

And yet the same sentiments of openness and leveling still exist among young publicists today, though times and media have changed. They share news and opinions via screenshots and videos, reaching young people who may be thinking about and discussing politics for the first time. And they're succeeding, thanks to today's social media.[8]

An important difference between them and me, now and then, has to do with how those media let you reach the public. Now that algorithms organize everyone's timeline and decide who's at the top, there's no longer any question of leveling in the technical sense. We know that radical profiles get more attention than introverted bloggers. All voices are allowed to participate, but only some are amplified. The algorithms serve profit, not something as old-fashioned as "content."

Aspirations change alongside technology. It's not about networking but views; what counts is not access to the establishment but impact. The blogger has become an influencer, writers have lost to shareholders, and individuals to commerce. However, you could also argue that the pretender, who sought to invade the establishment's stronghold, has given way to the activist, who strives to make the world a little better.

Of course, the idea that the blog era was a level playing field is a myth. There, implicit rules and norms prevailed just as much. And though I mourn the exchange of "Inhalt" for "content," it is a thing of the past. We can't go back to Neverland. This is not to say that nothing should change, nor that regulating tech companies wouldn't be a good idea. But even if the industry is regulated, the openness and sense of freedom and access will not return, simply because it's no longer avant-garde but mainstream now.

▶ ▷ ▶

I don't want to forget what it was that once inspired my love. The internet has given countless voices that were barely audible the opportunity to speak up, including those of women, ethnic minorities, and populists who say things of the kind "you're not supposed to say out loud." Voices grew into movements and action groups on all sides of the political spectrum. Lest we forget, there was Occupy and the gatherings in squares from Istanbul to Kyiv, and the protests that came to be known as the Arab Spring. These movements didn't bring what was hoped for and fought for to the death. Oftentimes, quite the opposite. Yet I cannot fully renounce the liberating power of technology, which has also brought me so much personally, even if the internet and politics have taken a different turn.

It isn't strange that those voices have shaken up the dominant order. It also isn't surprising, though regrettable, that the response lies in repression. The more voices that are heard, the greater the chance that someone will hear something they find unpleasant. Some people stop listening altogether. This even happens under the guise of freedom of speech, as with Elon Musk, who had the terms "cis" and "cisgender" censored on his own platform.

What has also changed is the issue of findability. If you want to be heard, it's best to parrot the opinion leaders who set the tone of the debate. A few dominant topics—and endless ads, links to online stores, and AI-generated content—have faded out an entire galaxy of fascinations. "Searching" is now a matter of selecting recommendations on YouTube, Spotify, or TikTok. Good luck finding anything.

Ironically, the more everyone can make themselves heard, the fewer individual voices actually resound. In a fit of procrastination, I searched for "cue cards." Surely someone, at some point, had written an ode to the rectangular note card with a red line on top. But even with noncommercial and privacy-friendly search engines, I only found stores selling paper. Until I tried Neeva, a so-called "content-driven" search engine. It gave me exactly what I was hoping for. I read about the only cue card Martin Luther King dedicated to Spinoza, about autism-friendly architecture, and even about translating Chinese poetry—one of my all-time favorite subjects. However, retrieving these articles is no longer possible, because a few weeks after my discovery, Neeva was acquired by an AI company. The articles have been sucked a little further into the black hole of the old web.

▶ ▷ ▶

"Unheard voices": by now that primarily signals name-calling, fake news, and hate speech. While the loudmouths get the most attention, the dissonant chorus of all those crazy interests and niche websites slowly dies away: a chorus that could make itself heard through technology and that is disappearing thanks to the evolution of the same technology.

All those voices, movements, protests, conversations: first I want to applaud the fact that they have had the opportunity to rise, before criticizing their message. I want to hold on to the internet's groundbreaking possibilities. Anyone can publish! No more fruitless waiting at the gates of the established media, but "Hello, world!"

It sounds naive and privileged, I know. After all, the breaking open of the public sphere, which was once revolutionary, has ended in a culture war. The revolution is over. That means we need to ask different questions. If the participation of all these voices in public debate is a theoretical fact, what are the practical implications? What is the post-digital answer to the digital breaching of communication structures? Now that everyone can speak, who is listening?

A LISTENING EAR

Tall, thin, steel legs support a dozen rectangular speakers made of concrete, from which undefined noises are heard. You have to enter the circle and bend down close to a loudspeaker to discover different sounds in the rumble: voices speaking an unfamiliar language, ambient noise, a vague pounding.

The latter turns out to be a heartbeat, recorded among the women featured in the art project *Oyayi* by the Filipino collective Kwago.[9] The recordings were made in a women's prison. The voices are those of inmates reciting poetry, amid the murmurs of the densely packed crowd. Sometimes the sounds swell into a drumming din. The heartbeats, voices, and prison space are the instruments in a composition that listeners can never fully absorb.

Kwago uses technology to create a positive listening experience. Listening, says the collective, is political. Visitors are invited to turn their ears to voices that are different from their own and that they don't normally hear. The voices do not tell a clear story or communicate a clear message.

Standing within the ring of loudspeakers, you are made part of a place.

Who's heard and who's not, asks Kwago? How can you give those unheard space to make themselves heard, in such a way that you don't speak *for* them, silencing them again? Watch out for the phrase "to give a voice to," as if privileged people—or media, platforms, and algorithms—are being so kind as to allow someone to speak, for which they should then be grateful. Rather, those voices were already there, talking, expressing opinions, and sharing insights, but no one has bothered to notice them.

These questions have been around for a while. "Who speaks? Who listens? And why?" bell hooks asked in 1994, for example.[10] An implicit call to the environment of "new voices," which, as noted, are not new to and in themselves. A call to the dominant order, though it isn't always clear who belongs to it and who doesn't (yet). For this reason alone, every speaker should also be a listener.

▶ ▷ ▶

In the circle of loudspeakers, the answer to the question "who listens" is clear: I am. At this moment, I have the privilege not only of making myself heard, but also of leaning toward the concrete box and silently, attentively letting the sounds flow into my ear.

What do I do, what can I do, what are we able to do—those of us who enter this literal circle as well as our figurative social circles? These are ethical questions that go beyond the call for representation. They speak directly to me, as a listening ear. They address the relationship between me and the crowded world out there. Listening immediately establishes a relationship: it builds a bridge between the one listening and what is listened to, whether it's another human being, nature, or one's own inner voice.

As with all political and ethical questions today, the question of listening is related to technology. How you position yourself in the world and how it presents itself to you—that is, your relationship with it—is profoundly affected by technology. More specifically, listening relationships are *mediated* by technology, ranging from sophisticated sound equipment to social media, and technologies understood more broadly, such as conversation techniques or musical improvisation. Technologies can facilitate listening, as in Kwago's work, or hinder it.

Listening, then, requires not only goodwill but also infrastructure, and today's infrastructure prioritizes other things. It propagates speaking rather than listening. On social media, value is created when people voice their opinions, and it's multiplied by how loudly they speak. The act of listening is difficult to share or sell. Sound doesn't always have a visible source and dissipates before you know it. To catch it, it helps to remain quiet and immobile, but in stillness, there is no data. In tech logic, listening gains value only when it conforms to that logic's conditions, such as visibility, growth, and engagement. In short, listening is valued once it becomes an expression. But in that case, it doesn't have a lot to do with listening anymore.

▶ ▷ ▶

Because technology mediates relationships and thus impacts our being in the world, design is a form of applied ethics, argues philosopher Peter-Paul Verbeek.[11] The same can be said about how we use technology. Platforms, networks, and devices establish a certain relationship between humans and the world (just as art installations like Kwago's do), but so do I. Relationships are never static, something happens between the things that are connected. In the same way, something happens in listening. Composer Pauline Oliveros, who developed the practice of deep listening, has called this the "listening effect": the act of listening changes something in the world.[12] And that makes you responsible for how you listen.

While technology mediates, I, too, am a medium through which sounds travel, which I try to decipher and then relay. A medium communicates with the dead, with what is absent and perhaps wishes to remain so. Similarly, as a listener, you're dealing with the spectral quality of sound. Its fleeting and even ghostly nature demands a heightened attention and an openness to that which cannot be represented.

Leaning forward with my body like a giant auricle focused on the voices echoing from the loudspeakers, I do not make them visible or measurable. I enter into a relationship with them. Listening is impossible without a listener.

. . . IN TIMES OF POLARIZATION

When I tell people that I'm researching listening, I don't primarily refer to the voices of Filipino women prisoners. I often add, even if it's only part of my explorations: ". . . In times of polarization." Aha! Of course, everyone understands that listening in polarized times is urgent, difficult, and important.

When politicians promise to listen, as, for example, Hillary Clinton and the Dutch prime minister of a right-wing cabinet, Dick Schoof, have done, it should at least partly be understood in the context of polarization. Public debate has hardened and supposedly nobody listens to one another anymore, but these politicians will set a good example by going on listening tours in the suburbs or inner cities. Who, then, is the one to listen to? Or, in the case of disappointing election results, who has not been listened to enough?

On the one hand, there are those who proclaim themselves to be "unheard," however loudly. They are the poles of polarization, or one of the poles. The idea is that for too long, discontent has not been listened to, while there are valuable lessons to learn. On the other hand, political listening focuses on "the silent middle," which deserves extra attention precisely because it's silent. The poles make so much noise that moderate voices are drowned out.

Regardless of which group is involved—and the distinction isn't always clear—I'm afraid much of this listening is performative. It seems to deliver a promise to act on what is said, but one does not follow from the other. In this sense, political listening is, and perhaps should be, noncommittal. After all, you can't promise to do something before knowing what it is.

Performative listening may be noncommittal, it is also morally charged. It implies that we would all be nicer people if only we listened to one another better, that it would prevent our falling for fake news and getting carried away so easily. And while I don't believe that listening is such a miracle worker (because miracle workers don't exist), for me, too, polarization is an important reason to peruse the subject.

I want to know how to escape the dynamics of hardening without becoming indifferent or turning away altogether.

And I'm not alone in wanting to know what listening can mean "in times of polarization." Countless books and articles discuss how listening skills can help with heated discussions across the kitchen table, at school, or in the office. They teach us that rather than responding to an unwelcome opinion with a sneering retort, it's better to inquire about the reasoning behind it. They advise us not to immediately come up with counterarguments or fact-check another person's beliefs, not to attach a moral judgment to a view with which you disagree. This doesn't just keep things friendly. In theory, open conversation will prevent antagonisms from deepening. Some authors say it's necessary to keep listening even if the other person has tumbled down the rabbit hole.[13] Conspiracy thinking often stems from real problems or wrongdoings, and listening would help us understand how such radical ideas emerge. There may even be a kernel of truth in what comes across as complete madness.

▶ ▷ ▶

The idea of listening as a miracle worker to combat social unraveling has been around for some time. Since the beginning of this century, the media has pointed its microphone at the "common man," to pick up the popular voice that it supposedly missed before.

One might wonder if that hasn't helped foster polarization. Giving attention to ideas and opinions allows them to spread further. Moreover, this form of listening is often preceded by suggestive questions that aim to confirm a predetermined narrative. Above all, over time "listening to" has turned into a matter of expression. It zeros in on individuals and their opinions, who are offered the stage but not engaged in conversation. The relationship established is often simplistic and crude, and thus, polarizing.

The line between providing a platform for certain voices and legitimizing or reinforcing them is blurry. Performative listening in politics and media erases the line even further. This form of listening often amounts to broadcasting, such as when an article or program relays the words of the person being "listened to" to the audience. It presents a dilemma for the individual listener. Is there a limit to listening? What if there is little or no "listening back"? Is reciprocity a prerequisite? These questions will recur in what follows, but I can already say that I believe that listening must strive to be limitless and unconditional for as long as possible—which is different from the idea that in politics and the media all beliefs should be given equal expression.

Without a basis of radical openness, I think there is no point in listening at all. You listen to hear something you don't know yet, and that includes where the limits to your listening are.

SELF-PROFILING

"What's on your mind?" is a Facebook original. A friendly invitation to share your thoughts that has turned into a rampant spectacle of opinions. Musk's platform asks, "What's happening?!" It sounds like the smiley face with its tongue out and one eye shut, as if it's saying, "Suppose nothing is happening; then that must change immediately!"

So what's on my mind? I have no idea, but I can think of something? What I say out loud, however, is rarely what I'm actually thinking about. What I'm *really* thinking is difficult to capture in an on-the-spot response. I often think of nothing at all or twenty things at once. While musing on the question, the moment passes. I'm always a bit behind online, and offline as well. Nevertheless, the invitation to share your thoughts or something that has happened hasn't been unwelcome. We are recognition-seeking creatures, and the demand for our thoughts is flattering. Just open your mouth or your laptop and report the first thing that comes to mind. The likes, and thus recognition, will follow.

But what should you do if you don't think anything? Do you just say nothing and disperse into "the silent middle"? Do you come back to it later, with your thoughts organized and carefully put into words, only to find that no one is interested in them anymore? Even if someone is, it will probably stay under the algorithms' radar.

I could never keep up with the constant reflection on breaking news, which was happening at one point especially on Twitter. I first realized this during the attack on the U.S. Capitol in Washington, DC, in January 2021. Commentaries and explanations from experts and "ordinary" people followed one after another in real time. I was speechless as I tried to process what I saw and heard. While I'm often grateful for the insights that others share during such times—though the shouting and grumbling easily drown out sensible reactions—I'll never understand how this manner of immediate responding works. So I say nothing. Nothing about the news, but also nothing about my latest publication or a book I read, nothing about the pernicious influence of social media on the formation of political opinions. I don't want to contribute to the commotion; I don't want to support the revenue model. Nor do I really believe that my opinions matter at times like these. I'm not usually very interested in the opinions of others, so why would they want to hear mine?

The question is whether this holds up. Doesn't my silence contribute to the problem of "interpassive" indifference?[14] Am I like the bystander who watches someone being robbed? Am I complicit in injustice if I don't speak out against it? In short, isn't speaking up a civic duty?

▶ ▷ ▶

Not everyone who shares their opinions so willingly does so out of a sense of duty, though. In an age that highly values visibility, it's just one of the ways to express yourself. On other platforms, it's less about your opinion and more about your appearance. Dwelling on your own face, or digitizing it as attractively as possible. There may not be that much difference. Opinion or appearance: both serve to profile the self. Visibility is one of the most valuable currencies now. If you're not visible or audible, you don't count for much.

This has a long history that is rooted in the Enlightenment and the invention of the individual and the political subject. However, the problem of self-profiling—culminating in what has been designated a society prone to narcissism—is also specific to this age and the technology that characterizes it. To function properly as money-making machines and surveillance tools, the online media require our cooperation. And we give it eagerly, whether with opinions or selfies.

EARBUD CRITIQUE

People "produce" themselves with the help of technology, writes philosopher Byung-Chul Han.[15] We strive to be seen and will use whatever means available. We're invited to continually multiply and re-create ourselves. Self-profiling is productive. What matters is sending, not receiving.

In addition to polarization and profiling, overstimulation is a feature of contemporary technology that hinders listening rather than facilitates it. We're in a state of total communication, with no respite from sending and thus receiving one message after another. According to Han, information lacks "temporal stability."[16] We live in a state of constant distraction and restlessness.

I also miss temporal stability when I finally gather my thoughts while scrolling, only to find that the momentum has passed. It's as if my perception and thinking are out of sync with the pace of the news and media. Always chasing behind the facts, I feel rushed and short of breath. Perhaps that's the point. The only adequate response to a "permanent frenzy of actuality" is to be constantly distracted, which then makes it even more difficult to take in information.[17]

This collective overstimulation did not develop overnight. Since Marshall McLuhan and the 1960s, it has been said that we live in a visual culture.[18] At the beginning of the twentieth century, Georg Simmel was already writing about the barrage of stimuli in the metropolis.[19] But there are always more possible assaults on the senses. Take a ride on the subway, for example. Already, you could hardly wait on the subway platform without seeing moving images, but now, in my hometown of Rotterdam, you're besieged by digital advertisements on the underground walls of the subway tunnels *between* stations. If you look away, you see the screens reflected in the opposite windows.

Sometimes I think the images themselves suffer from narcissism. "Look here!" they seem to shout. "Attention! Attention!" has long ceased to be merely a Buddhist call to worship.

Overstimulation, fragmentation, and acceleration go hand in hand. Images rush past you with the speed of the feed, the great equalizer bringing together conspiracy theories, job news, advertisements, online bullying, and wedding photos. Ideally, the length of a TikTok video stays under one minute, to keep the stream flowing and to continue capturing our fragmented attention within the screen's four sides. If a video or podcast takes too long, you should expect it to be played at double speed. Let's face it: if the explosion of stimuli comes to an unexpected halt, we quickly stir it back up ourselves.

▶ ▷ ▶

Images often come with sound. Played in public spaces they spill out their shrill noise. Of course, you can retreat to headphones, with or without noise cancellation. These "orphic media," as sound researcher Mack Hagood calls them, allow you to avoid being disturbed by the racket around you.[20] You no longer need to listen to what you don't want to hear since personal choice applies to the ear as well.

Orphic media, Hagood writes, give control over the outside world in order to create freedom for the self. A description that holds true for many technologies. But what does that freedom entail? Watching TV in public transport?

Listening to podcasts while grocery shopping? Or hearing nothing but silence while the outside world thinks loud music is blaring through your headphones?

Apparently, there are two kinds of stimuli: distracting noises that are better turned off and meaningful ones that I choose for myself. Is overstimulation then due to a filtering problem? Partly it is, I think, but not exclusively. The "noise" that needs to be "canceled" often comes from fellow human beings, which makes noise cancellation a morally charged technology.

Here, the problems of, on the one hand, self-centeredness and, on the other hand, overstimulation and fragmentation touch. Take the ubiquitous earbuds. First, they appeared in the streets, then in stores and in classrooms, and now they are left in during conversations. Earbuds put up a slim wall between the self and the outside world. In this sense, they act as a kind of pod for the whole person, a bathysphere of sorts that allows you to safely navigate the tumultuous outside (and inside) world. A personal safe space.

It's not surprising that we have a need for that. The fear of being humiliated or canceled after a thoughtless remark is not unfounded. As Hagood writes, in the persistent din of voices that is "diverse and democratic, yet overwhelming and often hateful," listening with discretion becomes a matter of "sensory and emotional self-care."[21]

This touches on the question of the limits to listening. Orphic tools make it possible to strictly guard the boundary between what you hear and what you don't. The border isn't open to be closed in case of need, but closed so that it can sometimes open. The risk of this, Hagood writes, is that the desire to hear only what you want becomes stronger and stronger, fostering "intolerances both sensory and political."[22] The elimination of annoying background noise expands from traffic to other opinions. We become increasingly allergic to what our ears don't like.

Controlling the environment to create freedom for the self can thus make the media user's self-centeredness grow further. Without considering others, you make yourself comfortable. In this sense, shutting yourself off with large caps on the ears and playing videos out loud on public transportation start to seem similar.

The fragmentation of information that causes one to seek protection from excessive stimuli eventually leads to fragmentation of a social or societal kind. This brings us to the core of "ear bud critique": people use audio technology to lock themselves into their own bubble in order to protect themselves, which increases loneliness and fragility in one and the same gesture.

For example, in an interview following her book *You're Not Listening*, journalist Kate Murphy states that "screens are guilty."[23] She describes us as being trapped in an isolated and lonely existence, with no idea of how to escape our self-imposed confinement. Listening is said to create connection and cure loneliness. And since lonely individuals are more prone to polarization, listening would solve two major problems of our time in one fell swoop.

This makes fragmentation, in both senses, a problem caused by others and to be solved by yourself. It's simple: attention can be trained, and ear buds can be removed (or put in?). You choose what you listen to, so the choice to want to listen to someone else is also yours alone. The tricky thing, as Hagood writes, is that orphic media offer freedom of choice but within the existing system. They turn a shared problem into an individual quest. You must optimize your environment yourself. At best, this creates the illusion of control. Either way, the outside world cannot be canceled.

THE BIG TSIMTSUM

Fragmentation and acceleration are ingredients in (social) media's paradoxical strategy to hold on to the attention they destroy themselves. They offer symptoms and treatment at the same time. The ingredients can also be used to deliberately divert attention from other issues. In his 2019 book *This Is Not Propaganda*, journalist Peter Pomerantsev describes how Russian rulers poured a flood of information into the world after the collapse of the Soviet Union, in order to render critical voices inaudible. While Putin employs a straightforward ban on certain words, this was a kind of reverse censorship, designed to drown valuable knowledge in an ocean of noise.

In a flood of meaningless information, one at most finds emptiness. Using a term coined by philosopher of art Boris Groys, who borrowed it from the Kabbalistic tradition, Pomerantsev refers to this phenomenon as "the Big Tsimtsum."[24] Tsimtsum is the moment just after the creation of the cosmos, when work is done and God retreats. The Big Tsimtsum also denotes the brief timespan after the Big Bang when—with a deafening noise that would be inaudible to the human ear—for the first time everything happened *not simultaneously*. Now it signals the dizzying cacophony of current events, ever increasing in volume.

▶ ▷ ▶

It's striking how the Big Tsimtsum, with its explosion of events and information, and the great void that is a complete lack of meaning echo each other. Everything and nothing touch. This invites us to think differently about what knowledge is and how it is communicated, and how to decipher messages in the chaos and distinguish signal from noise.

In the words of yet another tradition, the spiritual-analytic, what you need when you encounter a particularly dark spot is "a shaft of piercing darkness," after psychoanalyst Wilfred Bion.[25] To focus on something hardly visible, the more light you shut out the better. In other words, confronted with the unfathomable, you must dare to set aside theories and categories, the products of the Enlightenment by which we usually understand things. Answer darkness with darkness. The meaning that will then sound is a different one from the rational, analytical meaning we normally seek.

The dark ray thrown into darkness also implies the creation of a connection. A relationship is formed, even if it's based on not-knowing. It is a visual metaphor, though. What could be an aural equivalent? I choose a story whose evocation of the great void has haunted me ever since I read it. "The Great Silence" by Ted Chiang is explicitly about listening and the question of who is heard.[26] It's also about the Big Bang: "When the Arecibo telescope is pointed at the space between stars, it hears a faint hum. Astronomers call that the 'cosmic microwave background.' It's the residual radiation of the Big Bang, the explosion that created the universe fourteen billion years ago."

The title "The Great Silence" refers to the Fermi paradox, the question of why there is no evidence of extraterrestrial life despite the cosmos's vastness and old age. The story features a parrot, one of the last specimens of its species. The parrot reverses the perspective: the greatest silence is not to be found in the universe but here on earth. It is the silence of extinct species, a group to which the narrator will soon belong. He will disappear into history forever, taking with him a language, a mythology, a culture.

Meanwhile, the Big Bang reverberates. Why do we want to listen to that and not to what lives close to us? Shouldn't we respond to the emptiness of the Tsimtsum with an even deeper silence, like piercing the darkness with a dark ray? The story is like a mystical parable, its message at once clear and enigmatic.

A DIFFERENT COMMUNICATION MODEL

Let me recap. The internet has allowed countless voices to speak up that previously weren't part of the public debate. However, participation doesn't mean being heard. This raises the question of who is listening. There is the political dimension of listening that revolves around representation and power. Behind that dimension lies an ethics of listening. I am a being with two ears (and a heart), who is addressed by voices that call for my attention. I'm also a being who finds herself targeted within a polarized landscape. Challenged to speak out, pressed to form an opinion, and forced to pick sides.

To listen well you need to shut up. It helps to be curious about what's happening right in front of you and willing to give it space to unfold. By the way, in doing so, you also give space to yourself. Not the space of speaking, but of silence.

Sound artist Gordon Hempton says, "When I listen, I have to be quiet. And I become very peaceful. And I think what I enjoy most about listening, is that I disappear. I disappear."[27] That speaks to me. Or is this narcissistic again, as if it's my peace of mind that matters most?

In any case, it's not made easy. Social media is geared toward sending, not attentive reception. The same technology that encourages polarization is antithetical to listening. Information is produced and disseminated at an ever-increasing pace, in fragmented and dispersed forms that demand equally fragmented and dispersed attention. You're not meant to linger. The result is the emptiness of the Big Tsimtsum: full of noise yet bereft of meaning. Why, I wonder, would I ever take my headphones off?

▶ ▷ ▶

Metaphors shift attention. The same goes for models. Much of what has been described above echoes quite an old-fashioned idea of communication. The standard twentieth-century communication model is known as the "transmission model": a *sender* sends a *message* to a *receiver*. The emphasis is usually on the sender or the message, and rarely on the receiver. Philosopher and communications scholar Lisbeth Lipari writes: "Communication is thus understood as a mode of information transportation where we move ideas, like corn in a freight train, from one brain to another."[28] A major question in information science relates to this issue: How can we transfer units of information as efficiently as possible? The problem is, Lipari says, that "thinking of communication between people in terms of machines brings us before long to thinking of people as machines."[29]

Even in the twenty-first century, communication is often described in terms of transmission, a pipeline through which information flows from A to B. We know that this is not correct. There's no one-way street between the point of departure and arrival. The idea of information as a package containing a message—wrapped up, sent over, and unpacked on the other side—is by now obsolete. In the internet age, we are simultaneously sender and receiver, and in the network of pipelines through which information travels, we don't know where the message ends up or who will find, edit, or forward it. The idea of a message as an object with an ingrained meaning that is the same for everyone is equally outdated. The medium is the message. Information is open to interpretation: it's contextual and sometimes contested, disputed, fake, outdated, or groundbreaking. Both sender and receiver determine which adjectives apply. This makes the listener an active participant in a nonlinear process.

Lipari proposes a more holistic communication model in which the receiver plays a more creative role. A relational model in which speaking and listening intertwine and are mutually dependent. An ethical model, moreover, which also proposes a better way to communicate. Such a model isn't aimed at conveying information as efficiently as possible, but rather at opening a space for unpredictable encounters. It's possible, Lipari writes, "to think of communication processes as a kind of sharing rather than as a kind of sending, just as we might think of sharing (but not sending) a bowl of soup, a poem, or a beautiful sunset."[30] Communication is like a table where you sit down to enjoy a meal together—though online, we don't know who will come and join us.

▶ ▷ ▶

Sonologist Raviv Ganchrow is also interested in alternative communication models. He believes that the well-known transmission model is too linear for another reason. It's based on technologies such as the telephone and telegraph, which literally require lines, long cables over land and underwater. However, communication is also mediated by geology, chemistry, and the evolution of the earth and of our bodies, Ganchrow writes.[31] The specific formatting of sound waves and the shape of auditory organs or other sound receptors affect what can be heard. Communication, he says, is primarily atmospheric. There is a constant production of noise in our environment, and from that noise various signals resound. In this atmospheric model, listening means tuning into the environment rather than receiving a package containing a message.

Like the table at which we eat, space is something we share, with one another and with countless other creatures. In this model, animals, organisms, and places are connected and entangled, and they touch and influence each other. This requires paying attention to different types of signals and other forms of listening. The contexts in which communication takes place multiply, as do the participants. Moreover, in this model, the situation or environment itself acts as a medium that establishes certain relationships.

This expands the notion of who joins in communication and what functions as a medium. It also broadens the notion of technology. In addition to recording devices, dictation apps, noise-canceling headsets, social media, and AI, there are "analog" technologies that mediate relationships between listeners and who or what they listen to. A bowl of soup, a poem, and a sunset are all such techniques, just like the city bus, the questionnaire, and exercises in deep listening (which are discussed later). Finally, the listener—*me*—is also a medium that embodies and therefore helps shape relationships with others and the outside world.

LISTENING MACHINES

"Hey, Siri, tell me a joke." I didn't remember ever talking to a machine before, but my nephew knew all the tricks with the iPhone assistant. "Hey Siri, do a rap!" It reminded me of the artist Lawrence Abu Hamdan, who researched the infamous Saydnaya prison in Syria on behalf of the interdisciplinary research agency for human rights Forensic Architecture. In an interview, he recounts, "I would say Syria, and immediately Siri would say, 'how can I help you?'"[32] Machines listen, too, and they listen to us.

Of course, I have spoken to computers countless times. For example, when I'm asked to state my date of birth over the phone for verification purposes, or when I'm asked to confirm the arrangements just discussed with a clear yes. You could even argue that my voice talks to computers in my absence, since it has been recorded by dozens of call centers "for training purposes," which refers not least to training the computer.

Sometimes, this type of technological listening follows a simple transmission model, in which a receiving device picks up a message that we have sent. More often, it isn't entirely clear who sends and who receives in such mechanized listening. Although I may be the "sender," I still feel like I am on the receiving end, which is not usually the place where you want to be.

▶ ▷ ▶

Speech is the next step in the datafication of everything, according to communications scholar Joseph Turow in *The Voice Catchers*.[33] The voice is unique and deciphering it gives access to the owner's emotions and personality, much like an online data profile does. This can also be used in the same ways: for surveillance and for marketing.

With the growing popularity of devices like Amazon Echo and Google Home, Turow writes, we're getting used to having a listening ear in the house that can dim the lights, skip through music, and quickly look up facts. We know that these gadgets can always listen in on us. The fear of such voice assistants eavesdropping is justified. To improve the technology, employees check random recordings to ensure the algorithm's interpretation is correct. And why shouldn't a signal automatically activate when screams or certain words related to terrorism or drug trafficking are picked up?

Turow notes that, for some reason, we don't instinctively resist voice recognition as much as we do facial recognition. Could that be because of the spectral quality of sound? You can't see your voice, while your face acts as the mark of your identity. But the individuality and intimacy of the voice are no different. And, by now, even the bedroom isn't off-limits to the algorithmic ear.

These gadgets also familiarize us with the use of listening technology outside the private sphere. Smart doorbells monitor the street. The "smart city" listens to the noise in nightlife districts and to chants yelled in stadiums. More often than not, we aren't aware of it. In applications like these, the communication model is turned upside down. The sender doesn't call the shots; as the one being listened to, they become subordinate to the receiver.

▶ ▷ ▶

How do machines listen? To find out, Vietnamese Australian researcher Thao Phan reads a text aloud to a digital transcription tool.[34] Through this experiment, she aims to unravel how technology processes sound and meaning. The text she uses is the announcement for her presentation. The tool records her words and echoes them back in a robotic voice. On screen, the transcription of what the algorithm hears appears. Her own name in particular invites closer inspection: *tell phan, tack, Thao Phan, TFN, tell his, Taliban, taos, khalfan*. The transcription is correct once, meaning that her name has been part of the algorithm's training data.

This algorithmic guessing game is somewhat comical, but it's not that funny when the sound of your name is registered as "Taliban." Hearing "Syria" as "Siri" isn't an example of innocent miscommunication either. Such mistakes can land you on lists that seriously impede your freedom of movement. Phan calls this type of confusion of the algorithm "racialized misrecognition." The algorithm has a blind spot when it comes to other languages, names, and accents. The only way to deal with this is to learn how to interact with the computer, a form of "linguistic assimilation."

The surveilling ears in our phones and all sorts of devices, indoors and outdoors, are not necessarily searching for specific information from specific individuals. There's no secret agent hiding in the attic as in the movie *Das Leben der Anderen*, about the eavesdropping practices of the Stasi in East Germany.[35] Digital applications listen indiscriminately to whatever can be heard, looking for sound patterns wherever they occur.

Machine listening is data processing, using databases for pattern recognition. These databases contain not just letters or words but all kinds of sounds. For example, "AudioSet," a collection of sound clips compiled from YouTube videos (which means that uploading a video to YouTube advances Google's technology, whether you like it or not), divides sound into numerous categories, such as breathing, heartbeats, and speech, which may be shouted, screamed, or whispered. There are also bullet shots, sirens, and the sound of brushing teeth.[36]

It's important to remember that this auditory pattern recognition is deployed for specific purposes. On the other side of the machine there is someone who cares. In a conversation with a call center, for example, it could be about your emotions or creditworthiness. (How to determine that from a voice is the question, and prejudice seems inescapable.) The call center employee is provided with a ready-made analysis even during the call, ironically often in visual form. "All they have to do is look at a screen to see what the voice analysis is doing," says Abu Hamdan. "It's a lack of listening."[37] This extremely mediated, data-driven form of listening does not even require having to hear. In other words, the mechanization of listening renders the human relationship itself redundant—again, a law that applies to multiple technologies.

At the same time, it reveals what technology is not (yet) capable of doing. Machine listening wants clarity. It tries to calculate what is happening in order to apply the correct label. A cough, a clap, a shot. It needs to find the right category and cannot deal with what doesn't fit. Improvising isn't an option. Humans are better at that. It may be exhausting, but I can hold my own in a metropolis that bombards me with stimuli. It's as if I'm playing poker with the environment, all the time revealing and concealing. How it works is as opaque as an algorithm, and probably as flawed, but at least it leaves the door ajar for the unknown.

DISTRIBUTED LISTENING

We hear both a lot less and a lot more than we used to. On the one hand, we create highly personalized soundscapes (often at too high a volume) and, on the other, technology and science have vastly expanded the arsenal of audible sounds. Now you can listen to the Big Bang, to animal sounds from spectra that would otherwise remain closed off, and to all sorts of sounds that we have invented ourselves, from electronic music to the carefully designed click of a car door.

Technologies that amplify, record, or produce sound create new ways of listening. Consider, for example, the history of research into bird song, as described by historian of science Joeri Bruyninckx. At first, ornithologists had to use musical notation or other types of graphical writing to record bird sounds. Later, these could be recorded with the help of machines. However, to do so, the animal had to be placed close to, if not inside, the recording device. Today, it's possible to access vast or inhospitable areas with small recording units, which "autonomously collect thousands of hours of data that scientists can access remotely."[38] AI then looks for meaningful patterns in the material.

This practice can be termed "distributed listening."[39] It doesn't require a connection to what is listened to; proximity isn't necessary. Auditory perception is scattered over a large area, and you wait patiently for an encounter. The door is open to chance.

One risk of distributed listening is that severing direct relationships creates more distance from the object of inquiry. "It presupposes," Bruyninckx writes, "a nonhuman nature that can be studied by human listeners without being part of it themselves."[40] In that case, it's not a holistic or atmospheric model but an old-fashioned one-way street. The knowledge produced is considered objective but is actually an expression of a particular way of being in the world. In fact, an idea of being *above* the world.

This may be understandable when listening to birds, though knowledge falls short even in that case.[41] But the same applies when listening to people in the city. Although the recorded data are presented as neutral information, it brings its own perspective and is an expression of a worldview. It serves power and control.

A network of doorbells or voice apps can also be said to be a form of distributed listening. Devices and apps such as Amazon's Alexa or Apple's Siri, "smart" baby monitors, and security cameras listen autonomously and without a direct link between the listener and the one being listened to. The collected devices could be considered a kind of panopticon: you don't know if, when, and where you are being heard, nor by whom. Surveillance remains silent and invisible. Amazon claims that dealing with voice technology will encourage people to "adopt healthier communication practices with their loved ones and bosses," says Turow.[42] This educational effect seems nonsense to me, but the statement undoubtedly reflects the panoptic ideal.

▶ ▷ ▶

Can machines really be said to listen? That depends on your definition. Listening as an ethical act is beyond the capabilities of devices and algorithms, no matter how "smart." Yet they do perceive sounds in order to give meaning. Perhaps the way they do this tells us something about what "real" listening entails and the obstacles technology puts in its way. For example, if severing the direct relationship between listener and listened-to leads to a form of panoptic listening, it suggests that an ethic of listening calls for proximity and visibility. However, that would not be so remarkable an insight.

Metaphorically understood, distributed listening can also be a provocative exercise. It doesn't require you to be near the other person or to know in advance what you're after. It's mostly interested in nonverbal cues. What happens when you employ such distance, indeterminacy, and sensitivity to sound itself, as a human being listening to another human being? Could it be useful for dealing with polarization, self-profiling, and fragmentation?

The first step in distributed listening is finding sounds in places that were previously unknown, unreachable, or impassable. Distributed listening is listening outside your bubble. You are not the center and, indeed, there *is* no center. It's far from performative, and so offers a welcome exercise in curbing one's ego. It helps break down certainties and prejudices. Not knowing what it's looking for and seeking exploration rather than affirmation, distributed listening observes space and time, and values movement and change. What's noise and what's signal is less sharply defined. This creates opportunities to hear things that previously went unnoticed.

The most enjoyable lesson of distributed listening may have to do with fragmentation. Not only is distributed listening itself fragmented, but so is its specific way of hearing, with sounds split into snippets and words into phonemes. Fragmented listening makes you attentive to different sounds before they clump together into meaning. Say your own name out loud ten times in a row and it will sound like gibberish. The sense of alienation can put you on the trail of something new. The process bears resemblance to learning to read, which also starts with recognizing individual letters that must be converted into auditory sounds. Like with an algorithm, it begins with data, the content comes later. It is a form of "hearing with your eyes."[43] Learning this technique also makes you listen differently. The boundary between words becomes clear, which in turn helps you to recognize them. Even more joyful is the notion that singing can help with this process.

Again, this is an exercise in receptivity. By hearing sounds as plainly as possible, without expectation or assumptions, a new relationship to the content may arise. Because, if you already know everything, then why bother listening? The game of wanting-to-know and not-knowing-yet, of focused attention and open receptivity, will be of help once you return to other people, to "really" listen.

2
The Wish for Dialogue

VIGNETTE: PATERSON

In Jim Jarmusch's 2016 film *Paterson,* we follow a week in the life of a bus driver called Paterson, who lives in the place of the same name in New Jersey, a city where some of the great American poets have lived.[1] After finishing his shift, Paterson sets off for home, his metal lunchbox swinging from his hand. In a back alley of the bus terminal he encounters a little girl, waiting to be picked up. She stops writing in the notebook on her lap and reads him a poem.

Paterson listens. "That's a beautiful poem," he says when she's finished. He's not just being nice; he means it. After the girl leaves, he recites the opening lines to himself, word for word. He has paid careful attention.

The viewer knows that Paterson himself keeps a secret notebook full of poems. Throughout the film these poems appear on the screen one line at a time, as Paterson writes them down and reads them aloud. They are like the residue that settles from everyday life. It's not an enormously rich life, but that's okay. Paterson meticulously observes the smallest details and transforms them into meandering lines of poetry. He recites his lines for the viewer, but first and foremost, he listens. To the little girl, his wife, the bartender, the breathing of his dog Marvin.

▶ ▷ ▶

Who is this man who listens? Or, who can one be without sending all the time? Paterson has the soul of a poet or, one could also say, he's somewhat old-fashioned. He doesn't talk or move much. He doesn't speak up or flaunt his opinions. There are some hints of him being a veteran, but even that remains unspoken. Tellingly, Paterson writes with pen and paper. He resists digital devices, though that sounds too strong for his stoic character. He doesn't own a cell phone—he calls the smartphone "a leash"—and when his bus breaks down, he has to borrow a phone from a passenger.

The pen helps Paterson listen to his own inner voice, the poetic voice. But first he turns his attention outward. Free from digital distractions, he observes the world around him, unfiltered and in all its randomness. Of course, the pen and paper can also be considered a technology, and a fragile one at that, as Paterson learns when Marvin the dog gets hold of his notebook.

There are other "analog" technologies that serve as mediums through which Paterson listens. Take the bus, for example, which acts as a kind of extension of himself. Amused, he listens to the random conversations of the people seated behind him. The passengers talk about ongoing business and share random thoughts, doubts, jokes. The bus transports them from A to B, and the chatter that occupies them in the meantime jumps to and fro.

Or take the local pub where Paterson has a beer in the evening, and that's also in a sense an extension of himself and a medium for listening. While the bus is a world in motion, the pub is a resting place in space and time. The pub gives the floor to small and larger histories to unfold. People breeze in, only to leave again and return the next day.

The bus and the pub are both landmarks in a world that keeps on turning. You can be present and disappear again without much ado, sharing the space with others in the meantime. Paterson takes his place behind the wheel or at the bar and opens his ears, and his eyes, for that matter. He is a receiver of signals that he transforms into something else—words, lines, verses—through an inner and therefore opaque process. He's a medium, not really in search of something, but capable of finding.

The relationships that arise from this discrete, analog listening, do not seem very reciprocal. But that's not an issue for Paterson. You won't hear him complain or say, "No one listens to me." He is who he is, a bus driver–poet. And since he is who he is, others can be too.

ENGAGING IN CONVERSATION

It was a flash trend in the media a few years ago: columnists and presenters who engaged in conversation with their "trolls." Over a cup of coffee, the haters invariably turned out to be just human, not so much different from the media personalities themselves. Danish politician of Kurdish descent Özlem Cekic drank hundreds of cups of coffee with people who had sent her hate messages. "I had expected a horrible person—dirty, messy house. It was not. . . . And we had so many things in common. Even our prejudices were alike," she says in a TED Talk.[2] Prejudice and shortsightedness turn out to work both ways. The sender didn't realize that their hate messages hurt the recipient. And the one on the receiving end couldn't quite imagine that the abuse came from someone with real worries. Simply talking to each other seems to eliminate a lot of misunderstanding and negativity. But if it's as simple as having a conversation, why are hatred and polarization still so difficult to counter?

The format of the column or TED Talk will, to some extent, dictate conversational catharsis. Still, it's not surprising that personal encounters have a conciliatory effect. A conversational setting fosters a relationship that didn't exist beforehand. Apparently, it's easy for many to swear at a screen; the person on the other side seems less real or alive. Swearing is, by definition, not meant to be conversational but rather one-sided.

Does that imply that "real" contact through technology isn't possible at all? That seems too straightforward. For example, modern technology does facilitate conversation in projects like "Call Russia," initiated by Lithuanian Paulius Senūta following Russia's invasion of Ukraine in 2022. Russian speakers living abroad call random Russians via the internet and talk to them about the war, compensating for the domestic lack of reliable information. The Call Russia website provides scripts and questions that were prepared in cooperation with psychologists and other specialists. In practice, however, each conversation follows its own course, Senūta says.[3] Speaking person-to-person, something happens that eludes scripts and is ultimately unpredictable. In such moments, technology enables "real" contact precisely when it has otherwise been erased.

▶ ▷ ▶

Both the coffee drinker and the caller use conversation as an antidote to hatred and ignorance. In philosophy, dialogue is also often proposed as a remedy for conflict and polarization, both at the individual and societal levels. One example is the work of political philosopher Michael Sandel. He argues that we have lost the art of democratic public conversation. What passes for public debate today is mostly ever louder and harsher shouting matches from opposing sides, incited and propelled by the logic of social media. Or it's nothing more than a listing of technocratic arguments, preoccupied with details, and failing to address real questions. Hollow and empty as this is, is it any wonder that people stop caring?[4]

According to Sandel, public conversation should be about moral beliefs and principles, and the arguments that flow from them. Not in order to reach agreement, but rather to bring a range of values to the surface. These can then be collectively examined, without one of them having to win. The juxtaposition of different points of view is exactly what makes such an exercise democratic. Even in the absence of agreement, participants will feel more engaged.

The prerequisite for conversations about values and principles is that there's room for difference. Sandel himself is a master at providing such space, as he shows in his YouTube lectures. First, he describes an ethical dilemma and gauges the audience's ideas and opinions. Grouping and abstracting these, he then digs deeper and deeper to the core of the case. Rather than looking for definitions or decisive arguments, he lays bare how very different beliefs—such as those for or against positive discrimination, same-sex marriage, abortion, and other contested topics—often have the same starting point. People with radically opposing views may share the same values, such as justice or equality, but interpret them differently. Even if they never agree, they could gain a greater understanding of one another's position if they learn what grounds it—namely, a source as morally viable as their own.

Conversation, according to Sandel, can just as easily lead to less agreement. Although dialogue is an indispensable tool for democratic society, it doesn't lead straight to peace and prosperity.

▶ ▷ ▶

That's a refreshing perspective, because dialogue is sometimes presented as a panacea: a magic potion that makes everything okay as long as you drink it up together. Conversation among citizens is often regarded as the glue that holds a community together, more than a technique for connection, the path toward hope and trust.

Of course, it's more complicated than that. Philosopher Liesbeth Levy examined how public conversation was employed in the Dutch city of Rotterdam, first after the September 11 attacks, and then after the local party Leefbaar Rotterdam won the election and their lead politician, Pim Fortuyn, was assassinated in 2002.[5] After 9/11, with support from the municipality, "The Day of Dialogue" was organized. In 2002 followed the so-called "Islam Debates." The two events were diametrically opposed. The "Islam Debates" were emphatically not intended to be neutral, but rather to counter the "soft" and non-committal "Day of Dialogue." Instead of pacifying polarization, as the dialogues were intended to do, the debates galvanized it.

Dialogue and debate are often contrasted in this way. One is seen as focused on exchange, but the other on taking a stand. However, the dividing line is rarely so clear. Even in open or exploratory conversations, the structure of debate often pops up. We are by now accustomed to thinking about everything in terms of dilemmas and pros and cons. This happens even with Michael Sandel, when he looks for proponents and opponents of ethical dilemmas. Issues are first presented as black and white, with two opposing positions. But there are always multiple perspectives possible, which are easily brought to the surface by changing the context or citing concrete cases. Details or personal experiences can be added endlessly and will immediately complicate the distinction between for and against.

With its binary setup, debate is polarizing by definition. But even well-meaning, "soft" dialogue can turn out to be polarizing. Precisely because dialogue often concerns identity, beliefs, or culture, it can fuel polarization. Even if the goal is something positive, like understanding, connection, or exchange, if used at the wrong time, dialogue can exacerbate conflict.[6]

Nevertheless, dialogue remains a widely used and useful technique for meaningful connection. However, it's important to note that dialogue primarily organizes *speaking*. It may seem obvious that listening is also involved, but it's not. What it means to listen must be made explicit again and again.

PICKETS

We know that exchange consists of more than just speaking. Listening well is an indispensable skill for any moderator and often provides a difficult lesson for participants. There are countless manuals, methodologies, and courses on how to conduct a good conversation, all underscoring the crucial role of listening. A few key points keep recurring in these sources, like pickets that delineate the field within which the speaker and listener interact.

First, it's essential to establish and adhere to ground rules. Once the framework is clear, you can dig deeper. That is why Socratic dialogues, for example, follow protocols. Sometimes simple agreements suffice—that one is allowed to say everything, that you always let the other person finish talking, that you first repeat what the other person said before making your own point. In short, that you listen to each other.

Physicist David Bohm, who became an advocate of dialogue as a democratic and philosophical tool, held conversations with groups of up to forty people, which would surely get out of hand without rules. But with a good structure, he writes, "a coherent movement of thought, a coherent movement of communication" can emerge.[7] The emphasis on the coherent is interesting. Participants aren't merely exchanging information; they're building something new together. It's not the individual contributions that matter, but rather the collective result.

Bohm analyzes common errors in our thinking that you should try to recognize in a conversation. For example, we often place too much value on someone's initial reaction, which rarely conveys what's truly at stake. It's more likely an expression of automatic thinking habits and assumptions. And it's up to the listener to pick holes in those.

A good conversation that follows the rules of the game constantly moves back and forth between misconception and clarification, or, in other words, between difference and agreement. According to Bohm, what the speaker says and what the listener hears "are *similar* and not identical. Thus, when the second person replies, the first person sees a *difference* between what he meant to say and what the other person understood. On considering this difference, he may then be able to see something new, which is relevant both to his own views and to those of the other person."[8]

So the speaker is also a listener, who hears what they're saying via the other person's listening, which allows them to express themselves even better. Which again shifts the focus back to speaking, and away from listening.

▶ ▷ ▶

Another recurring theme in guidebooks for dialogue is empathy. Good listeners empathize with others. This is a key point in the work of psychologist Carl Rogers, one of the giants of dialogue alongside Bohm. Rogers is known for the concept of active listening, in which the listener's empathic capacity is central: "Basically, it requires that we get inside the speaker, that we grasp, from his point of view, just what it is he is communicating to us. More than that, we must convey to the speaker that we are seeing things from his point of view."[9]

You can do the latter, for example, by summarizing what is said or by simply adopting an open posture and nodding.

But how do you truly "get inside" a speaker? It's not obvious that you can adopt another person's perspective as if it were a pair of glasses. Or, using a less ocular metaphor, by standing in their shoes.

Empathy seems to be both a means and an end of active listening. It lets you tap into shared experiences regardless of differences, which ultimately will lead to understanding. However, simply departing from your own perspective is not recommended. To begin empathetic listening, you first need to swallow the response that is often on the tip of the tongue: "I have that too!"—which only leads to talking about yourself. It may feel like a show of empathy, but it's actually the opposite. You not only draw attention to yourself, but you also literally stop listening and start speaking. "Conversational narcissism" is what it's called.

But what if the point isn't to step into the other person's shoes and perceive the world from their perspective, but rather, to put the other person firmly in their own shoes, to help them adjust their own glasses? What if the priority isn't my understanding, but that of my conversational partner? In that case, preventing conversational narcissism becomes even more necessary.

I believe active and empathetic listening should work like this: You realize that you can never fully take on the other person's perspective, so you do your best to help the speaker understand things as clearly as possible for themselves, so that they can then share that with you. Your own understanding of the other person can only come after they have obtained it themselves.

▶ ▷ ▶

The one feature that is always mentioned in the ground rules for good dialogue is that as a listener you must "suspend" your own beliefs and prejudices. In other words, you must defer judgment on what you hear, at least for the duration of the conversation. Socrates already taught this.

So, in Socratic conversation, you keep insisting on the facts without expressing your own thoughts or feelings. This is sometimes called "empty listening."[10] You must empty yourself of yourself, of your empathic tendencies even. Indeed, empathy can turn out to be interpretation in disguise, not so much different from "I have that too!" A social lubricant that brings people together but also smooths out discomfort, and which might actually close off the path to insight and knowledge. In that case, empathy is the product of prejudice rather than its suspension.

When freed from preconceived ideas, dialogue becomes at best an empty and open space. For this to happen, however, its goal should not be predetermined. This means that if the purpose is to reduce polarization or increase mutual understanding, then there is no real dialogue. Real listening can only take place if purposelessness is at its core.

LEADERSHIP LISTENING

Every practice of attention gets its own perversion. Just as mindfulness and yoga have come to serve responsible and "self-caring" employees, listening has become a hallmark of modern, "human" leadership. It's the superlative of panacea, a one-stop shop along the lines of management self-help or "manifesting": master it, and success will come your way.

A humorous example can be found in journalist and Silicon Valley expert Dan Lyons's *STFU: The Power of Keeping Your Mouth Shut in an Endlessly Noisy World*. He calls himself a "talkaholic": his urge to talk was excessive and addictive. But he kicked the habit and learned to talk less and listen more. It has improved his life in every way imaginable: "Learning to shut the fuck up will change your life. It will make you smarter, more likable, more creative, and more powerful. It might even help you live longer. People who talk less are more likely to get promoted at work and more likely to prevail in negotiations." What more could one want? He continues: "Speaking with intention—that is, not just blurting things out—improves our relationships, makes us better parents, and can boost our psychological and even physical well-being."[11] "Speaking with intention": this reveals the true purpose of Lyons's silence. It's (again) really about speaking, in a way that gets people to listen better. Both him to others, and others to him.

I have come to call this kind of listening—which often begins and ends with speaking—"leadership listening." *Harvard Business Review* and *Forbes* have published dozens of articles in this genre with titles such as "In a Crisis, Great Leaders Prioritize Listening,"[12] "The Power of Listening in Helping People Change,"[13] and "6 Ways Effective Listening Can Make You a Better Leader."[14] Wait, so you only need *six* ways to listen *effectively*, and you will become a *better leader* as a result? Better leaders mean happier and therefore harder-working and more loyal employees. In such cases, wellness equals performance, just as yoga and mindfulness find their value in fit and productive employees.

Leadership listening means business. It's a way to earn respect and status. And though it could benefit everyone, it exists at a distance from the purposelessness mentioned above that dialogue demands. Above all, it's a skill that strengthens your competitive position, a building block for your resume.

At worst, this takes the form of performative listening—the same act politicians are sometimes caught doing. It looks good, but the question is whether it offers more than an attractive picture. In a handbook for employees of a large corporation, journalist Kate Murphy reads about Rogers's active listening, which is highly influential in the world of leadership and business. There's no mention of well-being or empathy. Murphy writes that it "focused instead on things like not appearing arrogant and keeping your lips pressed together while someone else is talking so you don't give the impression that you're about to cut in."[15] This reminds me of Simone Weil's students, who frown and hold their breath when they need to pay close attention, but mostly exercise their muscles in doing so.[16] I won't deny that I'm sometimes guilty of this, too.

THE OTHER, A SELF

How do you ensure that the other person is not merely permitted to come and play a role in your performance, but is given the space to be someone themselves? Someone who is more than "the other"—a category that, after all, is also the first step to dehumanization—and at the same time may remain "an other," someone who cannot be figured out just like that.

Even with good intentions, debate and dialogue carry the risk of othering. While we aim for understanding and connection, the other person may find themselves positioned as "alien." In that case, imagined contradictions are confirmed rather than addressed. Even if this "other" is approached not as a threat but as a fascinating stranger, the perspective comes from "us." It's one-way traffic and not a table at which we share a bowl of soup.

English professor Krista Ratcliffe shifts the focus from mutual understanding, which is a goal somewhere in the future, to what is left behind on the way there. Dialogue, she writes, is often seen as a dialectical process.[17] Thesis and antithesis lead to synthesis; in other words, through argument and counterargument a new understanding is reached. Ratcliffe points out that in such a process something is necessarily left behind, pushed away for the sake of synthesis. She calls this the "exiled excess."[18] It is that which we brush aside or talk over in favor of a unanimous conclusion. However, what we dismiss holds a great deal of information, such as our ideas about others and ourselves, and what does or does not have a place in the dominant culture. It contains the preconceptions that one is supposed to unearth and suspend.

In a dialectical process, agreement ultimately prevails over difference. This means that the "other" is encapsulated in the "same," and with that, listening ends. Can we continue carrying the "exiled excess" of conversation with us? Do we dare turn our attention to the dark places, where the light shines the faintest, casting a shaft of piercing darkness upon them? This requires, again, empty and open space.

Ratcliffe ultimately does expect something like understanding to occur, which seems difficult to reconcile with the idea that purposelessness is a condition for good listening. Perhaps the purpose should first be suspended, too, just like our expectations and assumptions. These are not all clear beforehand (after all, they are implicit or unconscious), but may surface during the conversation itself. The same may be true of purpose. Understanding and connection are never complete, finished, or even clearly defined. They will have to come alive in the process itself, in a kind of reversed Kantian "purposeful purposelessness." Letting go of the goal in order to work toward it; like digging up and hauling your prejudices before you can suspend them, or withholding empathy in order to be empathetic.

▶▷▶

Researcher Tripta Chandola puts this into practice in her ethnographic work in Govindpuri, a neighborhood in Delhi, India.[19] She employs listening as a scientific method to learn more about the inhabitants and their lives in the so-called slum. She doesn't just seek out their stories and opinions but turns her ear to all the sounds that can be heard. The soundscape of Govindpuri reveals the various political, creative, and repressed ways in which the local people live their lives. Often the soundscape is dismissed as noise, but Chandola tries to listen to it as they do. She listens to their listening.

Typically, the residents are the subject of conversation and not participants in it, for instance, when it comes to political decision-making. In other words, they have no voice outside of their neighborhood. According to Chandola, the locals aren't listened to primarily because they are not regarded as someone in possession of a self.[20] Instead of being subjects, they are objects: of scrutiny and policy, fear and loathing. In this case, the exiled excess is the self of the residents. Regarding them as people who are themselves listeners—and thus not primarily as speakers!—reverses this. It presupposes that they, like everyone else, have a self that perceives and establishes relationships with the world. Moreover, it suggests that they harbor an inner self in which all kinds of things can be heard that no one can fathom, and which is the source of a perspective and a way of being in the world.

Instead of stepping into someone else's shoes, you first must recognize that someone is already wearing them. And to echo the source of knowing that is that person, Chandola says, it is first necessary to mute yourself.[21] This requires some humility and the need to subordinate your thinking to the event presenting itself to you. Such listening takes place not only in your head, but in the world around you. Therefore, in addition to suspending your own (cognitive) assumptions, it requires opening up to (sensory) experience. In Chandola's words, "A sensual scholar needs to surrender to the world of senses—their meanings, their connections, their articulations and aspirations—humbly and patiently, without preconceived notions and prejudices."[22] We move from the table of dialogue to the din of everyday life.

▶ ▷ ▶

Pauline Oliveros said that listening to listening changes that which is listened to. This is the "listening effect."[23] Although it requires humility, it is also a potent tool that can shift positions of power. It implies a multiplication of the number of possible worlds and that creates potentiality and responsibility. Muting yourself, which is usually a sign of oppression or bitter self-preservation, can be a privilege. The question is how you choose to use it if you have it.

Or is this leaning too much to the other-as-other again? The underprivileged and unheard who are admittedly "somebodies," but somebodies who still need someone else to become subjects. I don't believe that is the case. Chandola's work shows that through listening, the whole idea of the poor, noisy, stupid, and intrusive other can explode into a multitude of individuals, who can be passionate, surly, interested, stern, or boring. Listening to the other as a self can turn out positive for them, but also negative. For example, if they turn out to be an undeniable bastard.

There's only one way to find out.

ROOM FOR THE UNEXPECTED

"It just sounds a little queasy," someone confessed when I asked him about his associations with listening. I hear you. I think that's mostly because societal dialogue always seems to convey a clear message. The message of peace and respect. Yes, we need to empty ourselves and suspend our preconceptions. We will realize how limited our own perspective is. Then, we are allowed to express our opinions like everyone else. When everyone has had their turn, democracy has triumphed.

Yet, in an ethical sense, dialogue is a hardcore phenomenon. Philosopher Emmanuel Levinas argues that encountering the Other is the beginning of ethics, indeed, the beginning of everything.[24] In the encounter, the other person makes an appeal to me that I cannot ignore. Although in Levinas's work it is primarily the face that reminds us of the ethical relationship that is the foundation of being human, speaking also plays a role. Listening, however, somewhat less so.

According to Levinas, in our daily interactions with others, we're mostly concerned with categorizing and absorbing what we perceive into "the same." We erase the other's otherness by fitting them into what we already know, our "totality." We let agreement prevail over difference. Instead of opening up to others, we literally and figuratively reduce them to a picture, through the image we have of them. "Imagining," in that sense, is problematic. Levinas, who died in 1995 when the internet was just beginning its ascent, would undoubtedly not care much for today's visual culture. At the same time, his description of the face of the other as the seat of humanity from which emanates a unique and undeniable appeal is extraordinarily visual.

In her discussion of Levinas's philosophy Lisbeth Lipari writes that in earlier work he has also called the voice a disruptive medium.[25] But whether it's the face or the voice that demands a response, when the emphasis is on answering, listening is easily forgotten. For the response, in turn, will be speech. "It is necessary to speak," Levinas states in an interview. The shortest answer sounds, "After you!" (In the interview, Levinas says, "After you, sir!").[26]

Levinas places ethics within the process of speaking itself, distinguishing it from the solidification into content.[27] "Saying" is of higher importance than "the said." Only sustained saying does justice to the infinite that is the human being. But this relegates listening, which should come in between appeal and answer, to the background. Wouldn't it be better to stay quiet, before we take the floor? Could listening in silence not be a response?

Perhaps, Lipari suggests, it's not even a matter of the Other first making an appeal to which I then respond—perhaps the act of listening, or a receptive attitude, must precede all that. In other words, maybe appeal and response cannot even take place without listening. Put yet another way, perhaps listening is what fundamentally makes an encounter possible. With a beautiful phrase Lipari describes this as "listening others to speech."[28] This would be a "maieutic" form of listening, in which the listener, like a midwife, allows speech to be born. Not "After you!" but "For you!"

A listening that precedes speaking recalls Levinas's notion that the ethical relationship precedes everything else. This makes listening an ethical act par excellence. Again, it's difficult to conceive of such a listening, which responds to the not-yet-said, as anything other than open and empty.

▶ ▷ ▶

Encounter creates space, yet space also seems to be a prerequisite for encounter. In the in-between—a term from Martin Buber's philosophy of dialogue—something meaningful and disruptive can happen. It's a space to explore differences together, without immediately exiling that which does not fit.

It remains complicated how to organize for the unexpected, just as it seems almost impossible to consciously suspend one's implicit—that is, unconscious—biases. But an in-between space, in both the physical and temporal senses, seems indispensable for both these actions. This is especially true in a highly mediated world that leaves no room at all for the unexpected. Frictionless streams of images spew preprogrammed affirmations; scripted talk shows and fuss-filled social media cut off the unpredictable. Totalization seems inevitable and listening before speaking unthinkable.

Of course, it is equally true that the media enable contact with others and bring them closer. But even then, the question remains whether individuality and otherness are allowed to exist, or whether they are brought back to familiar categories. As Byung-Chul Han argues, aren't online media an "Inferno of the Same," characterized by the absence of difference?[29] And if media really are an inferno of the same, does that mean that we as visitors and users are doomed to stay there? Or does that let us off the hook too easily?

Levinas teaches us that nothing absolves us of our responsibility for the other. I make up one end of the relationship and am therefore indebted to the other, whether I like it or not. The relationship is fundamental, and we cannot escape it. It's up to us to say "After you!"; to begin with "For you!"; to leave the in-between space open. Buber, whose work I encountered on a monastery retreat far from the mediated world, writes, "To begin with oneself, but not to end with oneself; to start from oneself, but not to aim at oneself; to comprehend oneself, but not to be preoccupied with oneself."[30]

I read these words as a breathing. The chest rises and falls, expanding and retreating. In between, there is a space. I also interpret them as a description of how listening comes before the other's speaking. How you should listen to the voice of the other as it resounds within you. The "exiled excess," the residue that can never be fully fathomed, also lies within yourself. If the other is a "somebody," then who am I? "*Je est un autre,*" as Arthur Rimbaud writes.[31]

TRACING THE KNOWN BACK TO THE UNKNOWN

A dialogue—unlike a debate perhaps—isn't like a tennis match in which two players hit a ball back and forth, with the one who scores the most points as winner. Or, in terms of the transmission model, in which a sender and receiver constantly change positions, a message box smoothly moving from one to the other. Dialogue complicates that model on all sides—at least the dialogic principle does. This is the principle of the infinite in-between, where exchanges between speakers and listeners, messages and media, language and the world, are made without beginning or end, as if it were one big, unstoppable feast. To my ears, at least, that is what dialogism as described by Mikhail Bakhtin, the twentieth-century Russian philosopher and writer, sounds like.

According to him, exchange isn't limited to people but is inherent to language, thought, and consciousness itself. We breathe in and out the other, culture, history, words. Breathing is not merely transmission, it is holistic, atmospheric play. The other flows into me, and I flow out into the world. It's an unfolding in time and space.

The word I breathe out has always already been breathed in, according to Bakhtin:

> The word in language is half someone else's. It becomes "one's own" only when the speaker populates it with his own intention, his own accent, when he appropriates the word, adapting it to his own semantic and expressive intention. Prior to this moment of appropriation, the word does not exist in a neutral and impersonal language (it is not, after all, out of a dictionary that the speaker gets his words!),

> but rather it exists in other people's mouths, in other people's contexts, serving other people's intentions: it is from there that one must take the word, and make it one's own.[32]

Language, and thus thinking, speaking, and listening, is a social phenomenon from the start. There is no such thing as a single voice, meaning, or identity. They are all necessarily ambiguous, or, as Bakhtin calls it: polyphonic. Here, we move from empty listening to full listening, as we moved from "After you!" to "For you!"

▶ ▷ ▶

What we call a "dialogue" often seems to be a series of monologues. One waits for the other to finish speaking, so you can speak yourself. Bakhtin's polyphony, however, understands dialogue differently. The audience at the tennis match seems to silently follow the ball without participating, but it was there before the players even entered the court. The rules existed before any of them were born. And all of them yell from the tops of their lungs.

You can effortlessly recognize this fullness within yourself if you listen to what is going on inside. We often call it the inner voice, but it is actually an inner "saying." Internal dialogue, where thoughts unfold and from where our speaking and listening arise, always contains other voices. Rather than a linear model, we are dealing with a tangle, like a ball of wool after the cat has played with it. Moreover, the saying in your head is connected to the saying outside; words are connected to other words; past to present to future. This tangle of relationships also implies that power dynamics are at play. Some voices sound louder than others.

We listen to some and less to others (and often we listen most to the unfriendliest ones).

Dialogue wasn't innocent for Bakhtin. He lived and wrote during the Soviet era and was all too familiar with the language of power and the power over language, including censorship, exile, and worse. But just as importantly, the voices silenced in such a tangle do not disappear forever. Polyphony is inherently rebellious. If meaning is dialogic and voices can be amplified or filtered out—constantly fed and in turn feeding—then everyone can join the game. Even those in power have no control over language. There is no one, true, authentic voice—neither theirs, nor mine, nor society's.

The thing is, if you demand that polyphony be given space from those above or below, then you yourself must endeavor to do so. Not necessarily by speaking, but by giving room and listening.

▶ ▷ ▶

Subversiveness also means allowing what does not fit into boxes to run wild. Bakhtin's profound interest in the grotesque should be understood in this context. Humor and caricature, filth and excess, express an ambivalence that doesn't leave power uncontaminated. They make a closed system impossible. Thus, the "exiled excess" is given a central role in dialogism. Or rather, a decentering role, because excess—the polluted, unintelligible, alienating, and nontotalizable—is everywhere. In me, in others, and in the language we use.

Polyphonic and decentered "saying" has no end; it is "unfinalizable," as is human being.[33] This implies, again, a certain openness and infinity that we must respect. True dialogue, according to Bakhtin, has no denouement, no final word, and does not lead to agreement. This doesn't mean that understanding and community cannot exist. Indeed, the dialogic principle fosters their existence. However, as soon as dialogue reaches a conclusion, it ceases to be dialogue. It is infinite or it is not, as are humans.

All well and good, but how can we put this into practice? I borrow the following maxim inspired on Bakhtin: The unknown should not be reduced to the known, but the known traced back to the unknown.[34] Isn't that what listening is all about, whether empty or full? Tracing the known back to the unknown . . .

A PHONE CALL

You had to dial a number and would then be paired with a stranger, someone who had called the same number at the same time.[35] The idea was that the two of you would talk for three-quarters of an hour, going in-depth with just some guiding questions and the other person's voice to hold on to. There was a protocol; the pickets were placed.

As a twenty-something, I suffered from telephone anxiety, long before it was trendy because it feels safer to text. On a landline you never knew for sure who would answer, whether the connection was good enough to hear them, and if they wouldn't ask questions you couldn't answer. You just couldn't be certain whether you wouldn't fail completely, as a human being.

Now I wonder if maybe I was afraid of the other in myself, which I couldn't hear well either. I was very good at exiling any possible excess, from somewhere deep down to even deeper.

This orchestrated phone call fulfilled all the conditions that had frightened me before, but it was presented as a work of art, thus offering an opportunity to transform my old fear into an aesthetic experience. As part of a performance in which hundreds of people would participate, failure was out of the question. I could already picture myself sitting there as a kind of diapositive of Marina Abramović—not a silent hostess at a table in a museum hall, but an invisible voice who welcomed the other, phone to ear. A kind of exposure therapy, artistic sublimation, and listening research all in one. You could say my expectations were rather high.

It's been a while since I've been to a party where you hardly know anyone and you're happy when someone talks to you, even if they mostly talk to you instead of with you. This was one of those parties and I was the host.

With well-timed chuckles and hums, I guided my telephone partner through the script. Suddenly I realized that my fear of calling had long been replaced by my perfected ability to defuse any social discomfort with wit and smiles. I was beset by the "hostess syndrome."[36]

In the durational performance called hostessing, I would surely win a prize. These were a long forty-five minutes of performative listening, without anyone noticing and without anyone giving a damn about my good behavior. No panacea, no catharsis. But then again, what was I thinking, who would seriously expect in an artistic performance to be connected to a—

LISTENING ≠ AGREEING

There it is again, the limit to listening. When you listen to someone, especially if it includes humming and nodding, it can soon feel as if you are agreeing with them. In any case, chances are the other person will interpret it that way. Why not just hang up and literally disconnect? The dictionary cites "obeying" as one of the meanings of listening for a reason. Like most people, I don't feel like obeying at all.

Stopping to listen can feel like a righteous lesson: Don't think I'll bow down to you! The problem is that the person who keeps yammering on most likely won't even notice. They'll find themselves interesting anyway, even if the listener does little more than sit there and nod obligatorily. Besides, I'm not interested in giving lessons. I have better things to do. As far as I'm concerned, ethics does not consist of punishments and rewards, issuing or collecting fines, credit scores, and bonuses, whether someone else's or my own.

If I want to become a better listener, I must be willing to do so regardless of who or what I'm listening to. Ethics demands unconditionality—I demand it. Too bad for me, because it's quite exhausting and we all know in advance that it will fail. But one thing is certain: it has little to do with obeying.

The dialogic principle teaches us: listening ≠ agreeing. Everything is there, whether you listen or not. You breathe in and out, and the air is never pure. But that doesn't mean I'm at the mercy of the toxic exhaust fumes of public debate. Often enough I wander off or descend into my own inner conversation. When you wander or drift away like that, you're no longer listening. But even if you keep your ears wide open in the fullness of polyphony, that doesn't mean you have to reach a point of understanding, whether for another or for yourself. You surely don't have to act on what the other is saying.

I find myself getting irritated by this limit to listening. The idea that you'll get hurt whenever you hear something annoying, the ongoing inclination to always relate everything back to yourself. Yes, listening is as much about you as it is about the other person. But turning it into a selfish endeavor is the opposite of what it's really about. If what you hear is so disturbing, why not put your fingers in your ears? There's always a chance, however small, that the other person's words will reveal something new. Whether for themselves or for me, as their words feed me. If that nourishment turns out to be poisonous, then no one can stop me from quitting and walking away, hanging up, or just thinking what I will. That too will teach me something valuable—namely, where I draw my own line of decency.

The problem with limits on listening is that they put conditions on the desired openness, freedom, and purposelessness of listening. And when something open, free, or purposeless is conditioned, it automatically ceases to exist.

▶ ▷ ▶

You listen because you don't know what's coming, otherwise it wouldn't differ much from algorithms looking for confirmation. Dialogue, with its swirl of voices, is a scene of friction that can develop into an "event," something that eludes familiar categories.[37] Such an event—an ethical moment if ever there was one—does not come easily to every dialogue. If the in-between space collapses and the different voices fall silent or if, in a more positive situation, the participants reach a synthesis together and exile the excess, then the event cannot unfold. When positions remain irreconcilable, nothing new can happen either. Voices become propositions and positions turn into formulas, as happens with polarization. In either case, the dialogue reaches a dead end.

This is why my phone call with the unknown man was a failure. He wasn't listening and, to be honest, neither was I. My inner saying took over. Should I have spoken up more, asserted myself, taken a stand? Was my humming a sign that a line was crossed? Did my silence get in the way? No, I don't want to end up championing speech like everyone else. I prefer to take my cue from Paterson, the poetic bus driver who often seems to think his own thoughts silently, only to turn them into poetry later.

Listening from a position of inner turbulence seems far removed from open, empty, and judgment-free listening to others. However, dialogue also takes place within oneself, within the language one uses, unspoken expectations, and cultural baggage. Even implicit prejudices can be understood as being thoroughly dialogic. This Tsimtsum of voices shouldn't be silenced.

Bakhtin points out that communication is broken in words and that the broken word belongs to communication.[38] This isn't necessarily a bad thing; it's just the way it is. Trying to smooth it over is counterproductive, so is ignoring it. Going full speed ahead may sometimes seem necessary, but listening silently is the option often forgotten. In the in-between space this creates, something new may emerge. Polyphonic silence can harbor relationships when speaking disrupts them.

IN PRAISE OF MISUNDERSTANDING

The question remains whether it's possible to empty oneself. I'm standing in this place on earth, with this history, with these ears attached to this body. I hear echoes of everything I've heard and learned before, just as this book contains a thousand echoes of all the voices that have contributed to it. Doesn't the dialogic principle say that our biases are part of us, of the air that we breathe? Isn't unbiasedness an illusion, debunked just like the so-called neutrality of data and algorithms? Algorithms are fueled with what already exists, and so am I. The cacophony roaring inside me cannot be turned down.

Being without purpose, muting yourself, paying attention to the exiled, leaving room for difference, beginning with oneself but not ending with oneself, tracing the known back to the unknown, polyphony, and unfinalizability . . . My own pickets delineate a field different from the traditional dialogue. This is rather the field of misunderstanding. But that may be an excellent starting point for good listening.

Understanding in the cognitive sense is often confused with understanding in the empathetic sense. And is the one really required for the other? For example, even with English as the lingua franca, particularly on the internet, it's hard to argue that there is less contention.[39] Perhaps the pursuit of mutual intelligibility is ultimately counterproductive, because it requires denying, erasing, or eliminating difference.

Lisbeth Lipari identifies misunderstandings as everyday moments of an ethics of interruption.[40] In misunderstanding, something happens that demands our attention. These moments are not empty but rather filled, with a variety of languages, unfamiliar sayings, unheard words, and misinterpreted facial expressions. The question is whether we dare leave our misunderstandings open instead of resolving them.[41]

▶ ▷ ▶

I suspect this requires an attitude of not-knowing, which is so important in psychoanalysis and Buddhism, as well as in art and science. Not-knowing is different from ignorance, which signals a lack of knowledge that can be addressed and resolved. It's also not comparable to deliberately maintaining an attitude of not *wanting* to know or looking away.

So how does one listen as a not-knowing person? In the book *The Wisdom of Not-Knowing*, I read about Theodor Reik's notion of "the third ear."[42] It's a concept from psychoanalysis (not for nothing called the "talking cure," with the analyst's silence serving as the listening treatment). The third ear doesn't grow on your back or out of your forehead; it's not "number three" in addition to the pair we already have. "Third" should be understood as that which doesn't fit into the binary boxes of one or two. It's the excess of these or perhaps the very relationship between them—between the listener and listened to. Similar to "the third eye," it has something to do with the kind of intuition that makes possible the new by drawing on the resources of the old. To tap into that intuition, you must first break through your automatic reactions and give space to unexpected associations. Intuition, I believe, is all too often confused with following what comes to you automatically.

Listening as not-knowing requires a heightened attention from the listener, without deciding what the attention is focused on. A fantastic paradox: being attentive without knowing where your attention is directed. This may also be what Wilfred Bion's earlier mentioned "shaft of piercing darkness" aims at. In the darkness you don't know what you're looking at, and in the Tsimtsum you don't know what to listen to. So you look with darkened light and listen from a cacophonous interiority. Distributed listening, but without the mechanization.

In another book also called *The Wisdom of Not-Knowing*, I read that the third ear points not only toward words but also "dreams, affects, somatic states, omissions, silences, thought sequences."[43] Silence, for instance, can be judgmental or condemning, shared, peaceful, or hostile. Attuning to this takes practice and requires examining your own dreams and affects, to acknowledge and see them for what they are: secondhand, incomplete, neither your own nor another's.[44]

It is a legitimate question whether listening with the third ear is not the forte of technology now: for example, in software used in the customer service industry to detect and interpret the emotional state of callers. If your voice sounds annoyed, uncertain, or willing to negotiate, you'll receive a discount or bonus, or not. Have algorithms, fed by our voices, characters, moods, and insecurities, neatly labeled and plotted out in patterns, not developed the best ear of all? Perhaps. However, this type of listening is for profit and deceit, not for the potentially liberating insight spawned by unexpected associations. Not-knowing can hardly be a method for technology's (and most of philosophy's) drive to want to know. One can imagine this kind of technology being used for purposes other than increasing gain, such as in a therapeutic setting or in an app for self-reflection. But the fundamental movement is the same. At its core, the unknown is traced back to the known, by employing automated interpretation.

The biggest problem with listening algorithms is that they ultimately take the place of the two ears with which humans listen, or four ears in the case of a conversation (although those who don't have a set of working ears can still have a good conversation). Both the listener and the person being listened to are replaced by it. In a technocratic world, humans are the exiled excess.

3 The Tradition of Testimony

VIGNETTE: TELL ME HOW IT ENDS

In *Tell Me How It Ends*, Mexican American writer Valeria Luiselli recounts her experiences as an interviewer and interpreter for children who have fled north from Central America, across the border to the United States.[1] Together, they go through a list of forty questions, ranging from why they came to the United States to inquiries about their families and home situations, and their journey through jungle and desert, by train and on foot.

It seems like a simple task, writes Luiselli: She interviews the children and translates the stories she hears into English. But as she listens and translates, she also imparts meaning at the same time. The latter takes concrete form when she has to categorize what is told. Every detail can be important in the refugee's plea for residency status. Prostitution, human trafficking, gang wars, and death threats help. But, of course, she cannot fill in the stories for the children.

Where runs the line between listening, translating, interpreting, and categorizing? The questionnaire itself does not respect such boundaries in any way. The forty questions assume a linear narrative that leads from A to B, which immediately puts the interview under pressure. "The problem with trying to tell their story is that it has no beginning, no middle, and no end," notes Luiselli. "The children's stories are always shuffled, stuttered, always shattered beyond the repair of a narrative order."[2]

The questionnaire turns out to be a technique that complicates rather than enables good listening. There is no open space here, only a gruesome game of hopscotch through which the children must pass, from one to forty. Falling is not an option.

▶ ▷ ▶

Luiselli inevitably becomes personally involved with the children whose stories she hears. Although she is supposed to act as a neutral conduit, she is a flesh-and-blood medium through which the voices carry and where they linger. She struggles to detach herself and starts to become obsessed, feeling at once powerful and powerless.

Several years after the essay, Luiselli published a novel on the same subject, *Lost Children Archive*.[3] She seems to have continued wondering how to ensure that these children's voices are heard. What do we need in order to be able to truly listen to them? Once again, she acts as a translator, now of the kind that transforms fact into fiction, perhaps even transcending that dichotomy. That, too, is not so simple. Luiselli explains how "it doesn't seem right to turn those children, their lives, into material for media consumption."[4]

As a witness to these testimonies, how can she pass on their experiences to the reader and in turn make the reader a witness to these children's lives?

A chain of testimonies unfolds in and between the two books. The minor refugees who are eyewitnesses to their own fate form the first link in the chain. Luiselli the interpreter then carries out a triple translation: from Spanish (which is their second language for some of the children) to English; from detail to category; and finally, from fragment to story. Luiselli the writer follows, molding her experiences into a personal essay and a novel. Books that make me, as a reader, the final link in the chain. At least for now, because anyone reading this becomes another link themselves.

Despite this chain of testimonies, the children remain alone in their trauma. It is one of the great frustrations expressed in the work: No one can carry the burden of the first witness. "Niemand / zeugt für den / Zeugen," as Paul Celan wrote: No one bears witness for the witness.[5] You can try to push a narrative into a list of forty questions, to categorize events, glue fragments together to present them to an audience, while it's already next to impossible to attach the first link to the second.

BEING PRESENT

New Year's Eve, 2006. With a loud rattling sound, I connect to the internet to look up the video of Saddam Hussein's hanging from the day before. How did I know one could watch that online? Perhaps from the newspaper or TV news. It took some time to find the recording including the ending (the *ending*-ending), but it wasn't super difficult.

According to Wikipedia, Iraqi state television distributed a video without sound after the event.[6] Hussein could be seen just before the execution and afterward, his body wrapped in a white sheet. Soon after, a video of the moment itself appeared online, this time with sound. That must have been the clip I saw. I wrote in my notebook: "Just watched the internet video of the hanging of Saddam Hussein. . . . 2 minutes 19 seconds. One of the last things he heard: 'Go to hell.' Such things really happen and can be viewed on the internet."

The disbelief that speaks from my note is by now as outdated as the term "internet video." I watched it at home alone via an internet cable and later talked about it with friends in a pub. I had a profile on the Dutch social network Hyves, but that was like a children's playground—the last place on earth where one would share such a video. The first iPhone was announced about ten days later. How many deaths have I scrolled through since?

I promised myself I would stop at that one clip. In the years that followed, however, it took as much effort to avoid seeing recordings of violence and death as it had previously taken to find them. Footage of a suicide bomber blowing himself up autoplayed in my Twitter feed. Links to decapitation videos of ISIS were shared with disclaimers about how horribly degrading those practices are, how horrible it *sounded*—really, it was said, *Don't click.*

There was a proliferation of footage showing police officers shooting or using force against Black U.S. citizens; videos that sparked a worldwide protest movement by being widely distributed. But there were also videos of fights provoked or staged with the goal of going viral. Online, we are all made witnesses to the suffering and sometimes death of others, whether we want it or not.

The word "witness" is ambiguous when it comes to the screen, which allows you to be in another place while you're at home. Even though you can't do anything, you keep watching. But what use does my scrolling thumb have to offer to the real eye and ear witnesses of history, who put their lives on the line to record and upload videos from war zones or protests?

▶ ▷ ▶

Much of what has been written about the ethics of listening touches on the theme and tradition of testimony. For instance, Zen master Bernie Glassman discusses the relationship between witnessing and listening in his book *Bearing Witness*. According to Glassman, bearing witness means being present without intervening or judging directly. One practical way to do so is to listen: "When we think we know something, we don't listen. We have to empty ourselves over and over, return to unknowing, and just listen. And listen. And listen."[7]

From the outset, this listening is an ethical act. It implies commitment. While Glassman talks about bearing witness to joy and suffering, it's especially important in the latter instance. That's another reason why it must be considered ethical. It requires reflection on right and wrong. Glassman has organized retreats for people of different religions and nationalities in Auschwitz, to be present together in what the Dutch poet and painter Armando has called a guilty landscape.[8] Glassman also held street retreats, to experience firsthand the lives of homeless people. These are acts that seek to spread goodness without intervention or judgment, yet that are far from passive, just like listening.

Dori Laub, a psychiatrist who worked with Holocaust survivors, has also written about the relationship between listening and witnessing, together with Shoshana Felman.[9] At the heart of this thinking is the idea that listening is an act that makes something possible—namely, testimony itself. By being present for the other person, they can tell their story. Testimony cannot take place without a listener.

Laub makes a distinction that is illuminating for today's media context. There's the witness who recounts their trauma and suffering, and there's the person who bears witness to this testimony by listening. The witness on the first level and the one on the second level are like links in a chain that can grow even further, like when readers or viewers take in the testimony through a book or film. When I read Glassman's book about his street retreats or watch interviews with war victims, I am, in Laub's words, "a witness to the process of witnessing itself."[10] Today, further mediation is added by social media, with all its commentary, algorithmic recommendations, and other kinds of reactions.

This implies that the witness chain simultaneously is a chain of technologies and media. These can support or obstruct both telling and listening, make other voices more audible or drown them out, insert the testimony into an existing story or break the story apart. I believe that the further removed one is from the first witness's direct experience, the more emphatically technology will make a mark.

Philosopher Giorgio Agamben points out that there are two words for "witness" in Latin, which I think also touches on this distinction between witness and witness-of-the-witness.[11] One, "superstes," means survivor, someone who has experienced an event firsthand. The other, "testis," can be understood etymologically as "third," someone who is present at another party's act, such as a wedding. In our thoroughly mediated "being present" to current events, these two meanings risk becoming mixed up. When I witness a catastrophe on my phone, am I a survivor or rather a "third"? Probably the latter, although sometimes I may feel like the former.

THE VIEWER'S PERSPECTIVE

Photo series of bombed cities in our news apps, violent propaganda shared on X, videos of torture and murder popping up in work or family chat groups: as someone who lives in the Netherlands, with no family ties to war zones or totalitarian states, I am mostly a digital witness to misery elsewhere, and often in a visual manner. Images in particular can make one feel like a witness, more than reading a report or analysis will. After all, haven't you seen it with your own eyes? And we see much more than we used to, thanks to smartphones. Sometimes against our will, when the news rushes at us at a pace that can only be matched with an extreme amount of screen time. You continue watching, even—or especially—when the images are shocking and keep you awake. You may feel obligated to keep looking at other people's misery, yet at the same time want to turn away from current events altogether.

Perhaps the difficulty of coping with the flood of photos, videos, and eyewitness accounts can be eased—while also made heavier, ethically speaking—by shifting the emphasis from watching to listening, as described by Glassman and Laub. My hope is that a listening attitude will provide a third option, deconstructing the choice between immersing oneself in the stream of images and turning off all the news.

First, though, we need to dive deeper into the stream of images that we continue to follow even though what we see puts us off. Back in 2003—that is, pre–social media—Susan Sontag wrote in *Regarding the Pain of Others* about the history of watching war images.[12] Why do we do that? For one, it makes you feel involved with the victims and their struggles. Additionally, we look for reliable information, and images, especially photographs, seem to provide exactly that. They shouldn't be too polished but show their authenticity. However, even if a photo looks authentic, there is always a choice in what is shown (and in what we view). The choice brings with it a certain perspective, as Sontag emphasizes. This was already true of the very first war photographs from the American Civil War.

When we think of war images now, they are likely to be moving images. But those have a history, too. One of the first political events that made a big impression on me personally, regardless of what my parents or teachers thought was important, was the outbreak of the First Gulf War in January 1991. (Perhaps that's why I wanted to see the video of Saddam Hussein's death.) At school, televisions were wheeled into the auditorium so that students could watch the events live. The broadcast was as authentic as it was propagandistic. The images gave the impression of a supposedly clean war, as Sontag writes.[13] The screens didn't show the dead and wounded.

Today, such images are available anytime, anywhere. We no longer need TV broadcasts to see what's happening in the Middle East. On our phones we watch alongside local journalists and residents, who film what they see, often from a first-person perspective or talking into the camera. Not infrequently, they are begging to be heard. This changes the relationship between the viewer and what is shown. Someone is speaking to us, inviting us to literally see the world through their eyes. You're not sitting at a safe distance studying photographs of someone who, as Sontag describes, "even when not an enemy, is regarded only as someone to be seen, not someone (like us) who also sees."[14] There's no doubt that the person filming and sharing their material online is themselves someone who sees. We look over their shoulders and watch the violence taking place before our eyes, even to the point of death.

As a viewer you coincide with the filmmaker, so it's not surprising that you feel like an eyewitness. The smartphone establishes a connection with the person living over there. However, it remains essential to distinguish between someone who bears witness to their own experiences and someone who witnesses them in turn through streams and social media. The screen brings others closer but at the same time keeps you at an unbridgeable distance. This is precisely why it becomes possible to watch, take note, and empathize in the first place: because you yourself are not in the middle of it. But such distanced experience is incomparable to that of the victim and shouldn't be confused with it.

It may sound uncomfortable, and it is. Sontag asks the harsh yet still relevant question what we actually learn from looking at photographs of the dead or wounded. Does it not primarily confirm our preexisting beliefs? Does the feeling of empathy that overwhelms you perhaps primarily help you cope with your own helplessness or even prove your innocence? If so, empathy risks becoming a performative form of witnessing, similar to performative listening. Although it makes us feel unpleasant and queasy from misery, it also gives us the pleasant sensation of doing something good.

▶ ▷ ▶

Media scholar Mareike Meis studies recordings of the Syrian Civil War, including what she calls "first-person videos."[15] These videos capture the moment when the filmmaker is killed by shelling or a bomb, for example. Authenticity is still a hallmark. The first-person perspective and the often blurry and jerky images make viewers feel as if they are present, over there. The middling quality of the images convince that the video doesn't come from the regime or state media, but rather from people on the street.

Her research led Meis to the depths of performative testimony. In the abyss of online war videos, she found recordings of torture and death and, even further down, reaction videos of YouTubers filming themselves while watching such recordings. These are also links in the chain of witnesses, although filming one's own physical reaction to the unimaginable suffering of others must be the absolute perversion of witnessing as an ethical act. It's the ultimate form of narcissistic attention-seeking that exploits others for one's own exposure and gain.

Nevertheless, it highlights a crucial point, according to Meis, which is that the same video can be viewed in different ways. It can serve as a distress call, indictment, or evidence of war crimes, but also as horror porn. The viewer's perspective is decisive. Therefore, as a witness-of-the-witness, one should examine the original context of the video as well as the context you place it in when you share or forward it. However, thinking from an ethics of listening, perhaps you should also try to let go of the context. Let the video speak for itself. Be present without intervening and without judging, without feeling the need to add anything to it. Above all, without refocusing the perspective back on yourself. Because usually, the spectator's intentions prevail again over those of others, of the witness at the first level.

SHARED IMAGES, SHARED RESPONSIBILITIES

How do those we look at benefit from our gaze? As Sontag writes, that gaze can reduce them to an object to be watched, which is taken to the extreme in reaction videos. It can also regard them as "someone (like us) who sees." Someone who has their own perspective and interiority from which they cast their view outward into the multidimensional world that surrounds them, in which they live. I'm reminded of the residents of Govindpuri whom Tripta Chandola approaches as listeners themselves. Can the gaze that glides over the screen, across images of pain and horror, also observe this inner perspective? Even if the person on view is no longer alive, we can try to think of them as someone who has watched (and listened) themselves. It will be even more devastating, then, that this perspective has been destroyed forever.

How to be a "good witness" specifically in a digital environment? Meis traces the algorithmic recommendations that lead to the horrific reaction videos on YouTube. The notion of virality, which has come to define the internet so strongly, makes the role of the viewer ambiguous. You cannot intervene in what you see, but you contribute to the spread of a video or message simply by watching or reacting to it. The receiver is not an end point, as in the transmission model, but an active node in a network. Watching means sending, too.

The megaphone effect of the internet, which automatically makes widely viewed content even more visible, leaves individuals with less control over images circulating online. But that doesn't make them less responsible. When an online object has already been shared thousands of times, your own view or click doesn't seem to matter, but each additional view or like contributes to its spread and findability. This applies to sexist or racist hashtags, also when they are condemned, to fake news, also when a disclaimer is added, and to images of suffering and death, even if they are shared to draw attention to injustices.

Therefore, responsibility does not evaporate online; rather, it becomes a collective matter that is shared by everyone who comes into contact with the message.[16] We're all links in the chain of witnesses. The fact that this is a collective problem doesn't absolve us from reflecting on our own actions. The shared responsibility of the entire chain asserts itself individually at each link. Pauline Oliveros has talked about the "listening effect," as previously mentioned; listening *does* something. The same can be said of watching. For tech companies and online propagandists, views are worth millions. For witnesses recounting their experiences from the battlefield, our attention can be lifesaving.

Many mediations are possible, and each in their own way allows us to engage with others and learn about what is happening. There are more options than being involved or looking away. The false opposition between loudly making your opinion heard, on the one hand, and dismissive indifference, on the other, must be deconstructed again and again.

WITNESSING WHAT'S GOING ON

What are your intentions for watching horrific images? And when do you stop? We follow current events not least because we want to influence them, Sontag said.[17] For her, this was true of the photographs of the war in former Yugoslavia. Only by knowing what is happening can you push for change. If everyone looks away from the horrors of a war, it risks being "forgotten."

Witnessing what's going on right now also happens in words: literature. Following Russia's invasion of Ukraine, Ukrainian writer Andrey Kurkov asked himself, "How do you write about something that isn't over?"[18] Writers feel called upon to report what is happening; it's expected of them. But like everyone else, they struggle when history becomes History. Are they able or permitted to write about other subjects, or should they (like everyone else) foremost participate in the frenzy of opinions? Novelist Tanya Malyarchuk recounts how people urged her to write something literary, like a story or a fairy tale. "I promised and knew it was an empty promise."[19]

The question of the role of writers and literature in this particular war is often brought up. Poet Natalka Bilotserkivets's response: "To me, that is like asking, 'What is the role of God in wartime?'"[20] Still, it isn't strange that specifically writers are asked about their role. In the first place, their profession has to do with giving meaning. The question also draws on literature's long history as a medium of testimony, particularly regarding World War II and the Shoah.

In wartime, every text is a testimony. And testimonies are not stories with a beginning, middle, and end. This is especially true when the events are still unfolding. The medium of testimony should reflect on that. And doesn't the internet seem quite suited for that purpose? After all, not only is it the place to stay in touch with the outside world when means of communication are scarce or cut off; it's also a continuous stream of fragmented reflections and documentation. Doesn't that make it a particularly appropriate place to write about what is going on? Ukrainian poet Tetiana Belimova explains how poetry on social media acts as an "instant response" to events.[21] In the process, she argues, technology exerts an influence on the message: lines of poetry take the form of "combat mantras," which begin to circulate beyond the online landscape.

▶ ▷ ▶

Literature provides not only battle cries but also comfort. In an interview, American poet of Ukrainian origin Ilya Kaminsky remembers how a friend replied when he asked how he could help: "'Putins come and go. If you want to do something, send poems. We're making a literary magazine.'"[22] Kaminsky exclaims, as if he can't quite believe it: "The country is at war and he's asking for poems!" Yet he himself is an equally firm advocate of poetry in times of war. It's what keeps you from going insane, he says, when you're in a subway tunnel waiting for the air raid sirens to stop.

In this way, the different links of the witness chain hook into one another as well in literary forms of testimony. Its function can shift constantly, just as the meaning of war videos can change depending on the context. There are poets and writers who experience war and violence and who may or may not write about it. There are the victims on the ground who find comfort or resolve in reading or reciting poems. Readers far away try to understand what is happening and may find solace in the words, but of a different kind from the one that those living amid devastation need. Last, language connects people to homes they've had to flee or cannot return to.

Clearly, one is more directly involved than the others. That said, even those who follow the news at a distance, safely and freely, though besieged by emotion and imagination, can be affected and engaged. The questions remain: What motive do you have for taking in the news? What do you expect to learn from it? How does the medium influence what you hear? How do you allow yourself to become involved? And what link are you in the growing chain? The role of the reader is as important as that of writers or poets.

In another interview, Kaminsky quotes a friend as saying, "The West is watching us. This war is their reality TV, and they are curious to see if we continue to live or die."[23] In that case, I understand one would rather have poems.

Reality TV is all about entertainment. You can respond with shock or sadness, with an indictment or a call to politics to take action. Or with a selfie, a joke, a "How Can I Make This About Me" post. Either way, it would be presumptuous to suggest that the grief of viewers is proportional to the suffering of those for whom war is a bitter reality.

In his 2019 poetry collection, *Deaf Republic*, Kaminsky holds up a mirror to news consumers. The poems read like a play in which the residents in a village silently rebel after soldiers murder a local deaf boy. In the poem "In a Time of Peace," the Western audience addicted to reality TV enters the scene: "I watch neighbors open // their phones to watch / a cop demanding a man's driver's license." We all recall videos like these. They don't end well. The cop shoots. "Into the car window. Shoots."[24]

We watch the violence on our screens, livestreamed while traveling, picked up on social media, and forwarded to group apps of family, friends, or colleagues. We hear the sounds that accompany it, bombs falling, cries of the wounded and displaced, of mourners.

"We watch. Watch / others watch," the poem continues. But the first to describe how he watches is the forty-something at the beginning of the poem. The verses let us learn how the poet watches, even if it's us he considers, as we in turn cast our gaze on another.

SUSPENDING THE TRUTH

There are so many ways to look and read—and listen. I want to revisit what Dori Laub says about the ethics of listening to testimony. An important theme he brings up is truth. In court, witnesses are expected to be faithful to the truth, but the (therapeutic) relationship between witness and listener should, at least initially, ignore the demands of truth. This relationship does not revolve around examining the facts or determining right from wrong. That would put the focus back on the receiver or listener. Instead, listening serves the possibility of testimony itself. As someone listens, whatever happened can unfold to the witness themselves. Only through the process of telling and being listened to can the witness learn about their experiences, which (being traumatic) may have been distorted, repressed, or partially forgotten.

The act of listening, therefore, precedes testimony and, consequently, the notion of truth. Unlike in a court of law, in an everyday conversation you must assume that the witness does not yet know the truth. And that's precisely why you must abandon any and all expectations and preconceptions. Laub describes the relationship with the witness as one of traveling companions: "Implicitly, the listener says to the testifier, 'For this limited time, throughout the duration of the testimony, I'll be with you all the way, as much as I can. I want to go wherever you go, and I'll hold and protect you along this journey. Then, at the end of the journey, I shall leave you.' "[25]

What does it mean to eventually leave the other again? Laub doesn't elaborate. Perhaps it indicates that when the testimony is over, the truth comes back into play. I also interpret it as a reminder that you can never really walk in the other person's shoes (even in first-person videos). There will always remain some unfathomable part, even to the witness themselves, and especially when it comes to traumatic experiences.

Laub writes about the travel companion's position:

> He needs to know that the trauma survivor who is bearing witness has no prior knowledge, no comprehension and no memory of what happened. That he or she profoundly fears such knowledge, shrinks away from it and is apt to close off at any moment, when facing it. . . . That the speakers about trauma on some level prefer silence so as to protect themselves from the fear of being listened to—and of listening to themselves.[26]

Putting yourself in this person's shoes means putting yourself in the shoes of someone who doesn't know yet what they're about to say, can't quite remember what they experienced, and are afraid to find out. The witness doesn't know what is true and what's not, because they don't know *what is*. Only by not seeking confirmation of facts and refraining from cross-examination, can the listener allow the witness to discover what was, through speaking.

In this way, the listener becomes a medium for speech. That makes bearing witness to someone else's testimony quite the task. But it also makes possible an event in the Bakhtinian sense. According to Laub, it involves "creation of knowledge *de novo*."[27] One could also name it the birth of a new perspective. The perspective of someone who is not only being seen but also sees, who not only has a voice but also listens.

▶ ▷ ▶

The potential of creation inherent in the relationship of witnessing is a reason why it's necessary to listen without appealing to truth, even when there seems to be no doubt about who is right and who is wrong. One might ask why you would suspend your so-called prejudices when it's clear who deserves support or when injustice is proven. Don't preconceptions sometimes simply reflect reality? If one is the aggressor, isn't it weak or even a form of complicity not to appeal to the truth? In a therapeutic setting, you might argue that perpetrators have a right to trauma treatment too. But don't we have other obligations as followers of the news?

An ethics of listening invites another way of thinking about this. First, there's always a chance that things turn out differently after all, or at least more nuanced than thought before. A second reason lies in the Bakhtinian event: only if we really listen and in doing so bring all voices into contact with each other, something new can emerge. And isn't that always our desire in conflict situations, especially ongoing ones, and even when the relationship between "the good guys" and "the bad guys" is crystal clear? Exposing wrongs, shifting public opinion, and forcing change all require an open space in which something can happen. Listening creates such a space, and starting to listen yourself is therefore the first step toward achieving it, even if you're convinced that you are right and prefer the other person to do the changing. This is putting the "listening effect" into practice.

Finally, any situation of injustice benefits from polyphonic witnessing, especially if the suffering is not only individual but also collective. A shared problem requires shared charges, even if they consist in multiple testimonies coming from the same side. Each testimony is different, and hearing those differences requires listening over and over again.

▶ ▷ ▶

An example of polyphony that resists clear-cut interpretation is the work of Belarusian writer Svetlana Alexievich. In her books, we hear the words of eyewitnesses of (Soviet) history, the voices of people who don't usually write history books, like women and children. All these testimonies come together to form one of the most impressive witness chains there are, from a writer who calls herself "one big ear."[28]

From each of her works sounds a multitude of voices. That doesn't mean that Alexievich herself remains neutral—quite the contrary. She, too, can be considered a travel companion. She spends hours, days, years with her interviewees, who often haven't told their stories to anyone before. While speaking, the women hear themselves for the first time: "I often see how they sit and listen to themselves. To the sound of their own soul."[29]

In the film *Lyubov: Love in Russia,* we see Alexievich at work.[30] I was curious about this glimpse into the Nobel laureate's listening practice. To my surprise, she turned out not to care at all about well-known rules for listening. Her interviewees repeatedly correct her after she poses a leading question. "No, I don't mean that," they tell her when she presents her witnesses of love with yet another assumption instead of an open question. It's clear that Alexievich enters into a relationship with her participants. She's involved head to toe and places herself on equal footing with them. In this sense, too, she is a traveling companion, who comes along to explore uncharted territory together. "I don't know," she says, when asked a rebuttal question about love.

CREDIBILITY

Collective testimonies that record unknown history; unheard voices that are finally able to tell their stories—here lies the power of Alexievich's work, but also of the internet and social media. Movements like #MeToo and Black Lives Matter can also be understood as collective testimonies that use and are mediated by technology. While Alexievich documented the stories of women, children, and soldiers, digital media provides an opportunity for anyone to do this on their own. The historical inequality of who could make themselves heard has been at least partially corrected. And that can be considered a significant event, though the backlash is substantial too.

A difference is that in the case of the MeToo movement, for example, the distinction between the witness reporting from the battlefield and the witness-of-the-witness who follows the struggle via screen isn't clear. Hearing testimonies about sexual violence or injustice inspired many to speak out as well. Listeners became speakers and the chain became a chorus, swelling into a societal-level movement of testimony. Moreover, the stories that emerged made clear that the line between what's going on now and what's in the past isn't always clear either.

▶ ▷ ▶

The disparity in who can or may testify about wrongdoings—and thus what qualifies as such—is known as "testimonial injustice." Philosopher Miranda Fricker's concept has to do not only with resources and media, but with prejudice too.[31] Stereotypes cause listeners to consider some people less credible. For instance, women are often considered emotional and therefore they aren't taken as seriously when addressing wrongs. Additionally, "hermeneutical injustice" occurs when someone lacks the words or concepts to make sense of their own experience. Sexual harassment is an example of this. There must first be a language for such an experience to be recognized and addressed.

The film *Women Talking* (based on a novel by Miriam Toews) provides an example.[32] A group of very religious, illiterate women discuss among one another how they will respond to the ongoing sexual abuse in their community. They know they are victims—of violence, incest, and rape—but they lack a framework of understanding. One of them puts it this way: "Where I come from . . . we didn't talk about our bodies. So when something like this happened there was no language for it. And without language for it, there was a gaping silence. And in that gaping silence was the real horror." They spend a day discussing what would be the best reaction: doing nothing, leaving, or fighting. They are in search of an outcome that does justice both to their suffering and to their moral and religious convictions.

Despite the terrible occasion, this joint search for meaning seems cathartic. Forced to examine and define their own values and boundaries as a group, they search for ways in which the incomprehensible events that befall them can retain a certain uniqueness. The unknown thus acquires meaning without being reduced to something familiar. This process is similar to what the term "MeToo" did for many people. It provided an outlet for something previously impossible to express, not to tame it but to give it a place in the world so that it could no longer be denied. It made them feel heard, often for the first time.

When thinking about testimonial injustice, the concept of credibility comes to the fore. Even if we accept that the exact truth is not important for the duration of a testimony, as Dori Laub says, we can exclude others by not valuing their words at all. Prejudice prevents us from even beginning to listen and makes it impossible for a relationship between witness and listener to develop. How should we deal with this? Should we not only suspend our biases but also correct them, in such cases? The question is how to judge when this is in order, who decides, and by what standard. Mustn't one first learn about the existing prejudices one has? In other words, can't you only correct your prejudices *after* listening? And then begin to listen anew.

IN THE JUDGE'S SEAT

An example of an entirely different order may illustrate why such a correction is important. It is the extremely mediated trial of actors and former lovers Johnny Depp and Amber Heard, who accused each other of libel following an article Heard published about domestic violence. The trial was broadcast live on U.S. television and had a parallel court of sorts on social media. A 2023 Netflix documentary reconstructs the case.[33] The series shows how it touches on a range of current issues, from fake news, image manipulation, virality, celebrity culture, and #MeToo, to misogyny and unevenly distributed attention. Audiences assiduously placed themselves in the position of jury and judge. Depp fared much better in this online court, while Heard was dragged through the mud of online feeds. Truth and credibility were constantly questioned. In such a case, unbiased listening seems almost impossible.

The documentary shows a chain of witnessing that is also a chain of mediations. Eyewitnesses tell their stories under oath in court; millions of people watch live; a few record reaction videos in the process and many comment via Twitter, TikTok, and Instagram; a year later, the whole thing is brought together in a Netflix documentary, which brings me as a viewer to the fourth link of the chain, witnessing a testimony about a set of testimonies. With each link, the story and its interpretations change. What really happened? What is the meaning of the statements made? Who's right and who's lying? These are questions with a deeper resonance in an era of post-truth and manipulated content. And that makes it even more important to consider what it means to listen to others while suspending the notion of truth.

Giorgio Agamben has noted that the ethical and the juridical are easily confused when thinking about witnessing.[34] In an age of social media and information overload, when people are pressured to voice their opinions and take sides without hesitation, this confusion is almost inevitable. The question of truth seems to have become both urgent and irrelevant. We've all turned into prosecutors and jurors. Obsessed with the facts, trained to judge, and ready to punish. Can we still suspend our judgment?

▶ ▷ ▶

The relationship between testimony and truth will always be complicated. In court, a witness promises to tell the truth under penalty of perjury. However, philosopher Jacques Derrida has argued that testimony always carries the possibility of inaccuracy.[35] A witness declares that they were present somewhere—they themselves, not someone else. This individuality makes the evidence provided unrepeatable. A witness's story is unique and can perhaps be supplemented, supported, or weakened, but not fully confirmed. If there were decisive evidence of an event, if the truth were plain for all to see, testimony would not be necessary. For this reason, testimony functions in a context of belief and trust—or disbelief and distrust. It has a "poétique" and "politique." Witnessing in a responsible way means being aware of the crack through which doubt flows in. The same goes for those who listen.

Testimony has an element of uncertainty even in the courtroom. Take the video and audio recordings used in the *Depp vs. Heard* case. They appear to provide "hard evidence," but the reliability of the images and audio, which were recorded with smartphones and therefore count as authentic, was a major point of contention. Photos, videos, and voice recordings can easily be manipulated. Even when they are not, they remain expressions of a particular perspective. The recordings themselves were far from unambiguous and had to substantiate memories and interpretations. But memories and interpretations are evidently poetic and political. This became clear in the parallel court on social media. Vloggers dissected sentences, examined the etymology of words, theorized about possibilities. Others addressed the unequal treatment of Heard and Depp, the role of gender, power relations, status differences. Although swearing and threats, memes, and hate videos dominated.

For many online followers of the case, the wish to influence the course of events, or their judgment, was a driving force. As long as the jury hadn't reached a verdict, any meme could potentially influence the outcome, right? Although it was prohibited for the jurors to check the media, it's virtually impossible that they heard nothing. Unbiasedness, that prerequisite for good listening, seems to have been impossible. For many, it was even undesirable. Bias was an explicit motivation for following the trial in the first place. And so it was polarized from the first moment to the final judgment.

POST-TRUTH LISTENING

Witness and listener carry each other, and are bound to each other. "Witnessing is essentially communicating, telling 'how it happened' to those who were not there, even if that seems impossible." An individual experience is shared with others. "As a result, testimony no longer belongs solely to the witness; the community of listeners helps shape and give meaning to it," states an introductory article about translated literature as testimony.[36]

If a testimony doesn't solely belong to the witness, is it then automatically at the audience's mercy, who can judge as they please? Or conversely, is the witness no longer responsible at all? This unfairly sets the speaker and listener up against each other, as if they were engaged in a polarized debate. Listening as a "third" party, as someone present, with an ear for the poetry and politics of witnessing, can break that polarized relationship. Just because there is uncertainty doesn't mean that truth is canceled out completely, nor that we have to take on the role of the judge.

The insertion of individual testimony into a collective whole also offers opportunities. Testimony benefits from a multitude of voices; this reinforces their credibility. Together, the voices create a space in reality where the events can land. Individual testimonies can then acquire a shared meaning and the relationship between the witness and the listener grows into a common narrative. But polyphony is a prerequisite for that to happen.

▶ ▷ ▶

Especially when something is still going on, and updates are continuously coming in on your phone, the urge to do something can be strongly felt. There you are, sitting in second or third row, and all you can think of is liking and sharing. Before you know it, you're participating in propaganda.[37] Keeping your judgments at bay can seem like an impossible task. The witness calls upon your trust and appeals to your morality. That cannot be ignored. But one need not exclude the other. Even if you respect a testimony's inherent uncertainty, listening is not an expression of indifference or denial. The listener is present; they stand by the witness. Is that also possible at a distance? How to be present online?

One way to do so is via "citation," writes media scholar Wendy Chun.[38] It is the practice of linking an event or experience to something similar from the past or present. This puts a testimony in a meaningful frame without overwriting it. Citation creates a polyphonic chain of witnessing that is maintained collectively. This happened with #MeToo. Loose tweets came together around a hashtag, bringing up more testimonies, on social media and in articles but also in conversations at the kitchen table, in the classroom, and at work. Past experiences took on a different color, and what was considered "normal" shifted.

Stringing testimonies together is not only something the witness can do, but also the listener. Creating space for different voices and their poetics and politics may be the greatest responsibility of the "receiving" side. Such a space shouldn't be a vacuum, but rather a meaningful and associative coherence in which different things coexist without having to arrive at a synthesis. Citation is an interpretive act without the accompanying judgment. In fact, it can reveal biases. As a great equalizer, citation can perhaps also correct the imbalance of testimonial injustice without it becoming an individual task. It raises questions of power and access: Who gets to speak? Who benefits? Who are you supposed to support? Questions of a completely different order than "Who do you believe?"

Digital technology is quite suited for this purpose. Besides resembling judge, jury, and prosecutor, social media is also a place where you can witness the world's stage and thus be present with others. This does require one to dwell on the multitude and the unknown, without reducing all those different voices and stories to the familiar as quickly as possible. To have an ear for both the common narrative and the uniqueness of a testimony that cannot be repeated or proven.

To this end, we can turn to art once again, where individual stories take on universal dimensions. Furthermore, art provides a variety of techniques for contemplating interpretation and uncertainty. Understanding how fiction works, for example, can inform our thinking about truth and credibility.[39] Literature in all its genres gives readers a sensitivity to the poetry and politics of meaning. It offers a training ground for suspending preconceptions and sharing interpretations.

This does require something from the writer as well. As an author of nonfiction, Peter Pomerantsev wants to show us reality. In an interview, he says that in post-truth times, perhaps the best way to do so is to show precisely the fragmented nature of what one can know about reality. "By creating that transparency of process, and showing the vulnerability and sketchiness of collecting reality, so much more reality emerges." Being on the receiving end teaches us how, "in order to understand the world, we should not construct a dichotomy of fiction versus realism, or art versus politics, but open ourselves to an assemblage of facts and fiction."[40]

Fact and fiction, Derrida would say, are also assemblages of each other. Maggie Nelson writes, "Mostly I want to point to third things—unruly, inscrutable, multivalent, un-ownable third things."[41] And fourth, fifth, and sixth things, I would add. There's plenty of room, online.

MATERIAL WITNESSES

Technology mediates testimonies and how we listen to them. However, technology itself can also become a witness. Artist and researcher Susan Schuppli elaborates on this in her work on the concept of the "material witness."[42] For example, she describes an old surveillance monitor from an Irish prison complex, on which the image of a corridor is still visible, even though the prison has long since been closed. The screen has become a material witness to the prison. It makes present what is now gone forever.

The monitor is a powerful visual metaphor. Are there also material witnesses related to sound and listening? An example might be the tool Thao Phan experimented with, whose algorithm recognized her name as "Taliban."[43] The database of sounds on which the algorithm runs can be understood as a material witness to our preoccupations, drives, and fears. Like the iPhone assistant Siri, which offered Lawrence Abu Hamdan help when he talked about his research on Syria.[44] These are nonhuman witnesses, with sounds "scratched in" like solidified memories of the recent past. They take the place of human witnesses and tell stories that are equally fragmented and incomplete. Sound is linked to notions of presence, truth, and memory in its own way. It shifts attention to nonlingual, preconscious, and embodied aspects of witnessing, and of listening.

▶ ▷ ▶

A poignant example can be found in *The Drone Eats with Me*, a diary about the 2014 war in Gaza. In it, Atef Abu Saif writes about the constant buzzing of drones that accompanies life in the war zone. This ominous sound becomes the hostile soundtrack of existence. "It's like it wants to join us for the evening and has pulled up an invisible chair," he writes.[45] The drones bring bombs and bullets, as well as psychic terror. A promised trip to the new ice cream shop cannot take place. His young son asks, "'But you'll take us when the *zanana* stops?' 'It's a deal,' I say. As I tuck him in later that night, I can tell he's keeping his ears peeled for the moment when the whir of the drones stops. He falls asleep, the shop stays closed, the drone hovers."[46]

"Zanana," Abu Saif explains, is a Gazan onomatopoeia for "drone." As you read on, the menacing buzz of the drone penetrates your ears. "The drone keeps us company all night long. Its whirring, whirring, whirring, whirring is incessant—as if it wants to remind us it's there, it's not going anywhere."[47] Meanwhile, on the other side of the border, a soldier keeps watch through an artificial eye. The drone is like a Peeping Tom without scruples. Its humming is part of its character; it can bridge long distances in time and space.

The drone's hum resonates with Lawrence Abu Hamdan's piercing project *Earwitness Inventory* about Syria's Saydnaya prison where prisoners were kept in complete darkness and silence.[48] Sound was one of the very few sources of information available to the prisoners. Using a variety of objects, devices, and technologies, Abu Hamdan reconstructs the sounds from the prison, based on survivors' testimonies. "The earwitnesses described, for instance, a building collapse as sounding 'like popcorn' or a gunshot as sounding 'like somebody dropping a rack of trays,'" he writes.[49] In a process of trial and error, Abu Hamdan and the ex-prisoners recreate these "acoustic memories" in audio clips. The excerpts can be heard online, alongside the transcribed testimonies. The clips let you listen to deep memories and traumas, etched into these witnesses' souls once and for all. The men are no longer there themselves; we have taken their place. It is a chilling experience of witnessing the testimonies of others.

Interestingly, the project not only provides an artistic representation of collective testimony, but also explicitly relates to juridical truth. Forensic Architecture, of which Abu Hamdan is a member, aims to investigate human rights violations using creative and artistic methods to bring perpetrators to justice. According to Abu Hamdan, these ninety-five sounds should also work as evidence in court. Auditory memories are as credible as eyewitness statements, he states. Sound is a medium of specific truth: the truth of memory.

However, even material witnesses shouldn't be denied the poetry and politics of testimony. A material or technological witness is no more neutral than a human one. When memories are mediated, bias is inevitable. Links in the witness chain can create strange loops and generate misunderstandings. Furthermore, both speakers and listeners are themselves mediums who influence the message, bodies that pick up and transmit sounds, trying to find meaning. Through bearing witness-of-the-witness, they make something happen.

4
Listening Practice

VIGNETTE: ON STAGE

Sound undulates along the walls of the concert hall, filling the space and vibrating through people's bodies from front to back and back to front. The stage is barely visible in the smoky, red-lit room. The shadowy figure producing such loudness from behind a high formation fades away against the curtains and in the stroboscopic flashes. I sit slumped back on a plush couch along the wall, trying with all my might to turn off my thoughts.

About three-quarters of the way through the performance, Pan Daijing steps out from behind her instruments, walks past them to the right side of the stage, and, standing in front of the loudspeakers, turns her back to the audience and stretches out her arms. It looks like a total surrender to the sound she herself produces, and an invitation to the audience to do the same.[1]

During an introduction to the festival where Pan Daijing performed, composer Remy Alexander had explained how, when we listen to music, we try to predict what is to come, based on the memory of what we've just heard. In that way, memory and prediction guide us through a piece. Experimental music, however, requires you to abandon the urge to predict and not to incorporate the sound into what you already know, not to shove it away if it doesn't fit within your expectations. I resolved to practice surrender.

How do you actually do that: listen? Not to other people, but to sound itself? Thinking about surrender is different from practicing it.

On February 28, 1927, British psychoanalyst Marion Milner wrote in her diary, "I lost myself in a Schubert Quartet . . . , partly by ceasing all striving to understand the music, partly by driving off intruding thoughts, partly feeling the music coming up inside me, myself a hollow vessel filled with sound."[2] Although a Schubert quartet is something different from experimental noise music, Milner's description evokes the same striving for surrender that I felt.

How does one become a hollow vessel filled with sound? In the red and smoky room with Pan Daijing performing, I sit on the bench along the wall with my eyes on the ceiling, away from the strobe. I try to open my body to the sound while at the same time keeping my mind focused on it. Not to understand—which would be to remember and predict—but so that I can take possession of the music and the music of me. The deep, vibrating sounds begin to scrape me out, layer by layer. I feel my torso take on the hollow shape of a vessel, ready to receive.

Things are going all right, for a while.

▶ ▷ ▶

Six months after the festival, I attend a performance by composer Huba de Graaff, who has been working in experimental sound art since the 1980s.[3] As the performance begins, the audience, scattered around the studio, closes their eyes. A deep concentration descends upon the room. Earlier, De Graaff explained how she collects sounds, some of which are found by chance and some of which she invents herself and then reproduces as best she can by other means. The chirping of a blackbird meets the metallic sound of a bicycle falling and so a whole new sound is created.

I watch the musicians and see how what I hear now comes into being. Then I decide to close my eyes, like the other visitors. Immediately I'm bombarded with images. An anxious mood sets my nerves on edge. The music suddenly becomes scary and menacing, like in a David Lynch film. Memories, associations, and physical affects wash over me. I see my mother, who died not long ago, before me.

I quickly open my eyes again. I look at the concentrated faces around me. What's going on inside all those bodies while they listen so calmly? I try to imagine the unheard voices of their inner selves, how they whirl, sigh, and scream, barely held together by the bodies sitting still on the benches.

Distracted, again.

SOUND AND IMAGINATION

When we listen to music, we oscillate between remembering and predicting. Can we let go of that? These words echo the ideas of others who emphasize that listening requires, above all, suspending one's preconceptions. After all, preconceptions are also a kind of prediction based on memories. Listening to music, then, might be a good exercise in battling bias.

It also helps us to notice more than what we see. Preconceptions often revolve around imaging. When I listen to someone, I have an image of that person in my head. This can be a metaphorical image, but it's often also concrete. Letting that go isn't easy. Even when I close my eyes while listening to a performance, images assail me. I can't seem to stop myself from turning what I hear into something visual, as if I'm a listening algorithm translating sound data into readable graphs.

When I think back on my mother's hearing loss, I see her hearing aid and the confused look in her eyes when she couldn't follow the conversation, I see her crooked finger, which she used to emphasize her own words even though they were always spoken loud enough. But when I think back to the last days in her house, I am overcome by a very calm silence; I had never heard it that quiet before. It was as if I had entered my mother's minimal hearing; it filled the living room like an invisible mist of anti-noise.

▶ ▷ ▶

In his book *Sinister Resonance,* David Toop discusses several paintings that depict the act of listening, or more specifically, of eavesdropping.[4] In *The Eavesdropper* (1657) by Nicolaes Maes, for instance, a woman exhorts the viewer to be silent with a finger on her lips. Around the corner of the stairs, a man and a woman are having a secret meeting. We must not betray her listening in. The scene immediately draws the viewer into a story that harkens back to a past and points forward to a future. It also has a spatial dimension.

The viewer stands on the threshold and sees everything but hears nothing, no matter how emphatically the act of listening is presented on the canvas.

Maes painted six scenes of eavesdropping. "All of them are different in quite subtle aspects but all depict this errant, suspect, uncontrollable, betraying, dislocating and uncanny quality of sound," Toop writes. "Moreover, they assume a listener, listening to nothing."[5] No matter how many whispers the painting evokes in the viewer's mind, it remains mute. Yet it is one of the few sources that provides an idea of what 1657 might have sounded like. For sounds more than a century and a half old, we rely on art, literature, and other circumstantial evidence. Even more recently, everyday sounds are rarely recorded. Therefore, listening to the past requires imagination, or to use a musical term, "fantasy."

It's a funny exercise to try to hear sounds when looking at images, instead of seeing images while listening to sounds. The first painting I heard when I saw it was Piet Mondrian's *Victory Boogie Woogie*.[6] I remember trying to put into words the experience I had in the museum but getting no further than listing musical instruments.

In such a case, what you imagine hearing is necessarily speculative. But that is actually true of all listening. Whereas in a painting you see everything but hear nothing, usually you hear all sorts of things that you don't see. Sounds coming from an unknown source, sounds so brief they could be hallucinations, sounds that disappear without a trace. You can never go back and replay them; time is inexorable.

All listening, therefore, is also a kind of eavesdropping. In *Sinister Resonance*, an empty chair that creaks while no one is sitting in it appears a couple of times. The creaking transforms a person's absence into a presence. It's not the person themselves but their absence that makes itself heard. A sound without a visible source is the ultimate uncanny phenomenon. According to Toop, the creaking even points forward to the end of humanity, much like abandoned buildings do.

A chair—yet another image. A mute image, that needs us to hear the speculative creaking and assign meaning to it. However, the extraordinary thing is that we can eavesdrop on a chair from a distance of many years and miles. For example, when reading the passages from Toop's book or Virginia Woolf's novel *Jacob's Room*: "Listless is the air in an empty room, just swelling the curtain; the flowers in the jar shift. One fiber in the wicker armchair creaks, though no one sits there."[7] For this reason, the listener themselves may again be considered a medium. A medium that communicates with what isn't present and that carries sound through time and space.

(UN)COMMON SOUNDS

Listening is super accessible and arduous at the same time. Sensitivity to sound develops as early as the mother's womb, and still, listening well doesn't come naturally. Even a short meditation will tell how much effort it takes to sit quietly and pay attention for a few minutes, and how many sounds usually go unnoticed. Apparently, it's not only difficult to listen to other people; "just" hearing sounds or tones is also hard. I believe the two are connected, that paying attention to the meaningless can make you receptive to the meaningful.

It also benefits our fragmented concentration. In *Quantum Listening* Pauline Oliveros recounts how she taught herself at a young age to constantly direct her attention back to the sounds around her.[8] It all starts with asking: What do you hear now? And now? And now again, fifteen minutes later? Listen to your own listening and suddenly you hear all sorts of things that previously merged into the background. On my way to Huba de Graaff's performance, I try it out. I hear a carillon chiming high in the sky, the roar of cars and the hum of air conditioners, the tinkling laughter of children on their way to the next adventure, and sudden silence, rustling with life.

It reminds me of the lockdowns during the pandemic. The streets, the city, and the skies were quieter. So you heard more. I remember how the sound of opening and closing the kitchen drawer struck me. That simple sound was somehow associated with a sense of freedom, because I was the one opening and closing the drawer, causing the sound to come to life, and no one could stop me.

While searching for sources about listening, I found several guides on how to listen to others, nature, and your body, as well as to all the everyday sounds in your home and on the streets. One guide recommended moving slowly around the room while making a recording with your phone. It suggested staying low to the ground in a corner of the room and snaring sounds in a web as if you were a spider, and invited you to keep your eyes closed upon waking and then deliberately opening all your senses at once.[9]

Websites such as Cities and Memory collected #StayHomeSounds, local sound recordings of the pandemic.[10] Artist Elise 't Hart composed a "Symphony for House Sounds," for which dozens of people contributed re-enacted sounds from their homes.[11] In *Engaging with Everyday Sounds*, music philosopher Marcel Cobussen writes about soundscapes that he recorded during the lockdowns, which made everyday sounds uncommon again. The unknown entered the all too familiar: "My encounter with the (sounds of) the trashcan-wind-pontoon assemblage already revealed the potentiality of the everyday as encompassing both the ordinary and the extraordinary, both the known and the unknown."[12] This sounds like a Bakhtinian happening, not between people but with things.

▶ ▷ ▶

Technology often plays a role in these types of listening exercises. It enables you to capture sounds before they disappear, allowing you to study them at your leisure. While Pauline Oliveros had to use an old-fashioned tape recorder, today almost everyone carries a digital recording device in their pocket that can capture sounds and create soundscapes. Creating such field recordings is a form of listening practice in itself. It helps train your attention, as for Oliveros, but it also helps you become aware of a multitude of perspectives. As sound artist Mint Park notes, even if sound is captured in a recording, everyone will hear something different in it, just as you can have a different experience each time you listen to the same piece of music.[13]

This richness of perspectives exists not least because sound resonates in an inner space. A space formed by memories and hopes, desires and fears. The sound itself becomes a memory as well. It transforms from a physical event into something immaterial that lives on inside you. Thus, external sounds are constantly in relation to internal voices. Listening can be called transgressive by definition—by making recordings, you capture the transgression. The goal should not be to freeze it in time, but rather to keep it alive and breathing, at every moment you play back the recording. In other words, the goal is not to take possession of the sounds but rather to enable a dialogue with them.

Or is such a focus on inner space too much centered on the self again? Not necessarily. The title of Haytham El-Wardany's listening manual *How to Disappear* implies that good listening is a kind of fading out. After concentrating on and paying attention to the noises around you for a while, you will blend into the background. Your body merges into the environment and the voices in your head fall silent. "You will find that the distance between yourself and the space's sounds has diminished, and that you have become part of the place," writes El-Wardany. "You will find that no one around you notices your presence; everyone will pass by without seeing you."[14] This sounds a bit like the listening of Zen masters, which doesn't seek to cross the boundary between inside and outside, but to dissolve it.

However, the dissipation is neither total nor permanent. The voice will resurface later, gather itself and, with some effort, rise up. It will make itself heard again and mingle with other voices. A bit like waking up after the darkness and forgetfulness of night and choosing to keep your eyes closed before opening them fully, transforming absence into presence.

TIME-SPACE CONTINUUM

In her final novel *Between the Acts*, published shortly after her death in 1941, Virginia Woolf presents a scene reminiscent of John Cage's renowned 1952 piece *4'33"*, in which musicians do not play their instruments for four and a half minutes, in order to allow—nonexistent—silence to resonate. Miss La Trobe, the director of the annual village play, also wants to give space to the daily silence-that-isn't-silence on her stage.

> Miss La Trobe stood there with her eye on her script. "After Vic." she had written, "try ten mins. of present time. Swallows, cows etc." She wanted to expose them, as it were, to shower them, with present-time reality. But something was going wrong with the experiment. "Reality too strong," she muttered. "Curse 'em!" She felt everything they felt. Audiences were the devil.[15]

That devilish audience doesn't get it! Unlike Cage's musicians, they don't realize they are part of the performance. To see the present and hear the silence, you have to pay attention. But they are distracted, most of all by their own thoughts. This also applies to Miss La Trobe, by the way; her inner space makes itself heard just as loudly.

▶ ▷ ▶

"Try ten mins. of present time" sounds like an exercise in deep listening. Pauline Oliveros's practice of Deep Listening (©) has grown into a polyphonous collection of listening techniques, especially involving the nonverbal. Sounds from nature, the sustained tone of an instrument, the echoes of voices in space, breathing, or wind. Exercises are written out in "listening scores" and "sonic meditations," around which communities, retreats, and trainings have formed.

Although such listening may seem direct and immediate, it's highly mediated by sophisticated, albeit mostly analog techniques. Oliveros points out that there are many ways of listening, and the technique you choose determines what you hear. The simplest distinction is between "global attention" and "focal attention."[16] At a workshop, deep listener Sharon Stewart lets participants, myself included, experience the difference.[17] Outside, we stand still, somewhat uncomfortably at first. Then we close our eyes and, under Stewart's guidance, listen to the environment. First, we let the floodgates open—global listening—then we follow a single sound—focal listening—then the floodgates open again, and so on. I especially notice that sound moves around a lot, whizzing from left to right, flying up and down, and disappearing into the distance. Noises swirl around us as we stand rooted to the spot like trees along the water's edge. Ten minutes of present time.

It is also possible to focus on remembered or imagined sounds. Take the following list inspired by Oliveros: Soft footsteps. Children giggling. A door closing. Water dripping. A dog barks.[18] Simple, ancient sounds that are deeply ingrained in human memory, by—yes, by what? Life and nature, songs and stories, as well as movies and commercials. These sounds reside somewhere in our minds, in our inner space. As soon as you hear them, the boundary between outer and inner world is crossed.

I'm reminded of the Mastodon account "sounddescription" ("random sound descriptions from movies and TV series"). Every few hours it lets a sound echo in your head: "[car honking]," "[muffled voices on TV]," "[machine beeping insistently]."[19] These artificial sounds we carry with us, too. They surface without effort. Understood this way, listening need not be complicated after all.

The sounds you remember exist in your mind, yet at the same time sound is a physical, bodily experience. It's immersive and four-dimensional. Where you stand affects what you hear, as does the passage of time. Inner space adds some more dimensions. You can position your ears in countless ways, which impacts what your hearing, even before you get down to techniques or scores. As you turn your head or move your body, you can hear, *feel*, how what your ears pick up moves along. It's like a reverse Doppler effect that creates the distorted howl of sirens chasing past you while you stand still. Moving yourself, you also distort what's echoing out there.

Deep listening in the here and now is thoroughly physical. It doesn't belong solely to the domain of the ears; the shoulders, heart, and belly participate as well. "I heard it with my back," someone told me after Huba de Graaff's performance. And although I couldn't imagine what that would be like, I believed him.

Hearing is not just for the ears anyway. After all, we feel the vibrations from sounds in the air. In her "Hearing Essay," percussionist Evelyn Glennie describes how she listens, as a profoundly deaf musician.[20] Her whole body participates in the process, from the indispensable lip reading to perceiving a range of vibrations through various limbs: "The low sounds I feel mainly in my legs and feet and high sounds might be particular places on my face, neck and chest." However, Glennie emphasizes that all listening, even by those with the best hearing, relies on picking up vibrations. That's why she calls hearing "a specialized form of touch."

▶ ▷ ▶

After the listening exercise outside, the workshop participants perform another of Oliveros's compositions: the "Extreme Slow Walk."[21] I've been looking forward to this, the absurdity of it. In the parking lot in front of the studio, we begin walking in slow motion. It takes enormous effort to move as slowly as possible, shifting your weight onto one foot and then taking a step forward like a clumsy yet graceful Big Bird, so much so that I completely forget to listen. Halfway through, with one leg in the air, I think of Oliveros, who constantly draws her attention back to herself. What do you hear now, and now, and now, a minute later? While keeping my concentration focused on my muscles, I try to prick up my ears. And then suddenly, it seems as if my ears are everywhere. In my toes, on the top of my head, yes, even in my back. The soles of my feet listen to the paving stones and even deeper, to the earth beneath.

Deep listening means perceiving as many sounds and tones as possible, from across the time-space continuum.[22] One complicating factor is that humans are part of that same time-space continuum. You will inevitably discover this when you slow down to the extreme.

NATURE SPEAKS

Many listening exercises, including those of deep listening, involve the natural world. Indeed, the fact that listening is in the spotlight today has as much to do with polarization as it does with the desire to restore our relationship to nature. But while polarization calls for interpersonal and verbal listening, nature calls for listening to the nonhuman and nonverbal. And though it has a clear purpose, this type of listening too necessarily begins with not-knowing, which can never definitively transform into knowing. Grasping nature once and for all is just as impossible as fully understanding the other or yourself—which is not to say that one shouldn't try.

Nature isn't typically considered a source of knowledge in its own right. Rather, our current relationship with nature is one of submission, extraction, and domination. We want nature to obey us and do what we want, as efficiently and profitably as possible. Or it's an object of inquiry, itself inert and lifeless. As the opening sentences of *The Mushroom at the End of the World* by anthropologist Anna Lowenhaupt Tsing state:

> Ever since the Enlightenment, Western philosophers have shown us a Nature that is grand and universal but also passive and mechanical. Nature was a backdrop and resource for the moral intentionality of Man, which could tame and master Nature. It was left to fabulists, including non-Western and non-civilizational storytellers, to remind us of the lively activities of all beings, human and non-human.[23]

Nature was always on the receiving end. But now it's our turn. First, because nature is making itself heard loud and clear and humans—like everything else—will not escape the consequences of a changing climate. Second, hopefully, because we are finally beginning to take the role of receiver seriously. Instead of treating nature as a resource without agency that we can do whatever we want with, can we learn to recognize it as a speaking entity that we can listen to?

This idea is not new. One of the first books to address humanity's destructive impact on the natural environment was Rachel Carson's 1962 book *Silent Spring*.[24] The title refers to the silence resulting from the mass death of birds and insects, which in turn is due to the use of pesticides. Although environmental pollution may seem abstract, it can be heard simply by listening.

For many communities, however, such listening has always been "natural," as has the sense of being in a relationship with nature—and not one of master and servant. In *Braiding Sweetgrass*, for example, biologist Robin Wall Kimmerer explains how for the Indigenous peoples in the Americas, a mutual relationship or rapport with nature is paramount. The "non-Western storytellers" that Tsing mentions have valuable insights to offer on this topic. So do nonhuman storytellers, says Kimmerer. Plants, trees, crops, and animals have inhabited this planet much longer than humans have. We can learn a great deal from their experience: "Plants were here first and have had a long time to figure things out. . . . What if Western scientists saw plants as their teachers rather than their subjects?"[25] By listening and watching—in other words, by closely observing—you can discover the knowledge that is "lived out" in their growth and flourishing. This begins with genuine curiosity. Kimmerer describes how she engages in conversation with the living things around her, asking not "What is it?" but "Who are you?"; not "How does it work?" but "What can you tell us?"[26]

Anna Tsing refers to her approach to inquiry as "polyphonic assemblage."[27] Polyphonic, thus, without proclaiming a singular truth, and assembled, so, composed and movable. As the work of both shows, listening takes place on several planes and often involves multiple steps. If you want to know what nature has to say, you can start by listening to those who have already learned its language. That's what Kimmerer does in her book when she shares the wisdom of Haudenosaunee, Anishinaabe, and Potawatomi tribal elders. They draw on many centuries of handed-down experience with the natural world in which and with whom they live. In turn, Kimmerer connects this wisdom to her scientific profession as a biologist.

Nature, I propose, is a witness too, that tells stories without a beginning, middle, and end, and from which a chain of testimonies unfolds, always handed down and therefore always mediated: by the scientific categories we use, by fables and stories, and by technology. Hearing these testimonies begins with opening the senses, which anyone can try. In the backyard, at the park, or on the beach.

▶ ▷ ▶

The "Embassy of the North Sea" explores how the voice of the sea can be represented in politics and jurisprudence. This has happened before with the Whanganui River in New Zealand, for example, that has been recognized as a legal entity since 2014. The first step in the Embassy's research is to listen, otherwise, one cannot know what the sea "wants" and how to represent that.

For most people who can hear, the sound of the sea is easily retrievable from memory, whether from personal experience or from movies or TV. Of course, that's not what the sea really sounds like. The sea can also be called a polyphonic assemblage. The Embassy writes, "What sounds do you hear on the beach? The roar of the surf, the whistling of the wind, a constant noise that swells and softens again, the hiss of the foam dissolving on the sand."[28] To most ears, these individual sounds will come across as a constant noise that is sometimes louder and sometimes softer, but mostly indefinable and meaningless. However, labeling something as noise often amounts to dismissing it as without value.

Unlike on a screen, different sounds heard while listening on the beach can't be distinguished, labeled, enhanced, and stored. That would be the scientific method, which is indispensable, but not the only one. On the beach, I'm part of the clamor. The sea presents me with a question that I must relate to. How long will it take before I discover something meaningful? Before I distinguish the cries of the seagulls, the splashing of beachcombers, the spattering of a branch on the waves, the dashing of a dog that jumps after it, flapping kites, screaming children?

To understand the sea, you need all your senses. When facing the superhuman forces of the sea, one must also exercise humility. On the beach, you are part of a larger context. Nature is not a backdrop for your main character fantasy but a participant in the conversation, moved, like us, by the dialogic principle. And at the same time, cutting through established avenues of communication, always retreating, never fully revealing. To decipher the stories it tells simply by existing, you need patience and curiosity, abandonment and discipline, a letting go of memory and prediction.

TECHNICAL REPRESENTATIONS

Obviously, listening to nature also happens with the help of technology. One example is the work of composer and ecologist Bernie Krause, who uses field recordings and soundscapes to document changes in animal habitats. Similar to Rachel Carson, Krause focuses on the connection between sound and biodiversity, or life itself. In a famous 1988 experiment, Krause recorded sounds before and after the so-called "selective logging" of a forest plot.[29] This new logging method, which involves cutting individual trees here and there rather than entire sections at once, was believed to have little to no impact on animal habitats. However, the recordings, and their visual translations, conclusively show otherwise. Even after such scattered logging, the plot harbors far less life than before.

This information is important and valuable, but the soundscape and graphics are first and foremost factual representations of a quantitative sound level. Can I be made to listen to the forest itself and not the information it represents?

In an artistic attempt to give the North Sea a voice, the "Language for the Future" project developed a language algorithm that allows one to "converse" with the sea via computer.[30] The algorithm converts noise into signal to make the nonverbal verbal. This is meant to destabilize the way the sea is talked about through language itself. Such "rewilded language" should at the same time rewild our relationship with the sea: less focused on taming and controlling, and with more room for the sea itself. The result is a "saying" full of neologisms and strange grammatical constructions. There is no trace of policy language—of poetry, all the more. This, too, is a representation, but one that fuels a different way of thinking.

Still, I don't know how I feel about the sea being given an algorithmic voice and thus being captured in a data-driven language, which is cast across the world by humans like a net. These technology-mediated voices of the forest and sea reduce the listener to just two ears attached to a head. Above all, they want to communicate with my brain. What happened to the rest of my body and all those other dimensions that are so important?

▶ ▷ ▶

I'm able to retrace it at the exhibition *The Art of Listening*, where I walk through a time-space continuum of sound that requires technological mediation as much as mediation of the body. Zeno van den Broek and Robin Koek's artwork *Raumklang* occupies an entire underground space.[31] There's nothing to see. Sounds linger in the air, waiting for someone to come and catch them. Wearing a backpack and headphones, I step into the dimly lit room and move through the sound architecture, searching for signals. The box on my back tracks my movements and sends the tones I summon into my ears via headphones. Over time, I discover all sorts of sounds around me—spectral creatures that I can snare in a web, but which also tend to evaporate in an instant. As I wander through the space, perching on my toes and bending my knees, I improvise a composition. My body is simultaneously instrument, performer, and audience.

It's both uncanny and intimate, and obviously a highly technological affair. Every sound has already gone through a chain of mediations before coming to play hide-and-seek here. First, the artists recorded the sounds in this exact location, then they returned them in processed form back to the space. In turn, I summon and assemble the sounds into a piece of my own, just like the other visitors who fabricate their own melodies. My body is an indispensable medium for making the sounds resonate. And although this involves a tracker on my back and a headset on my ears, the result is as multidimensional and physical as the extreme slow walk. I enter into a relationship with the space through the space I occupy myself, without reducing the unknown to the known.

TECHNIQUES OF ATTUNEMENT

There were, of course, always the birds. Their twittering first written down in notations on paper until technology made it possible to record it and later to capture it in distributed and automated ways, covering large areas and long timespans. Technologies that can be employed as much out of an urge to know as out of wonder. Composer Olivier Messiaen, for example, recorded birdsong so he could incorporate it into his work.[32] Using his tape recorder was the initial, technological mediation, but incorporating these sounds into music can also be considered a form of mediation, using highly sophisticated techniques of creation.

As an amateur birdwatcher, I'm stuck to the species in my inner-city garden. Sometimes I use my smartphone to record the noisy evening chorus, during which they seem to sing all at once, without noticing each other. But my recordings are only intended as reminders of a moment and not in any way as art.

▶ ▷ ▶

My favorite sound is that of the wind in the trees. Tall trees, and not too much wind. The sound should come from the leaves moving, not from the air blowing on my ears. As sound engineer Olivier Nijs says in an interview, "What's intriguing about wind recordings is that the wind is only audible in the things it touches and moves. Each type of tree has a different sound. Conifers are much quieter than deciduous trees. . . . A catalpa has thick, large leaves, and sounds coarser than an oak, which is more likely to rustle. Birches have smaller leaves than oaks and need less energy from the wind to be addressed."[33] It sounds like he is describing the various instruments available to the wind. I would like to learn to play them, too.

On a walk along a river in the countryside, I come upon an overgrown path at the foot of a dike. Two trees—poplars, I think—stand about fifty meters apart, singing a duet high up in the air. I decide to record them with my phone. First I walk back and then up the path again, until I'm standing right between the two trees. Then I turn from one poplar to the other. It's as if I am performing along with them. When I listen to the recording, I can hear the sound going back and forth between the trees, even through my phone's mini speaker. I zoom in on the leaves, each one swaying separately yet also moving all together in one fluid motion.

It makes me realize that I am a guest here. I walked up this path to find these trees that have been here for decades. I may be the center of my own world, but that's it. The trees are doing their own thing. I'm merely a witness. By turning around and walking back, raising my head and the phone in my hand, I change my perspective and with that I change what hear. It's like turning an object around in your hand to see it from all sides. Only I'm not holding an object; what I perceive surrounds me. I cannot listen in a distributed way; I can only listen situatedly.

▶ ▷ ▶

If we are to relate to the world in a meaningful way, we need techniques in addition to technology. Like those of deep listening, field recordings, and music. Plus entirely unique techniques discovered through listening itself. Philosopher Ike Kamphof did this in relation to her chickens. How does one listen to the animals that scurry around the backyard, laying eggs? Kamphof began by focusing her attention on the chickens' rhythms: "I had to learn how very important it is for chickens to go to sleep at a specific time indicated by their bodies. . . . Human mechanical time says little about their biorhythms. As long as they depended on me as chicks to reach their roost, I had to learn to listen to their bodies, the slowing of their pace, their habit of brushing their feathers together one last time."[34]

In short, she learned to attune her own rhythm to theirs. Such an alignment succeeds only if you use your whole body. The same goes for Kamphof's second technique, which is mimesis, or "an inner imitation"[35] of what she observes in the chickens. In the soles of her feet and hands, she tries to imitate the typical way a chicken puts her legs down. This inner imitation leaves any simple form of hearing far behind.

So does the last listening technique Kamphof mentions, "reciprocal articulation."[36] What really interests the chickens (besides food) and how can their owner play a role in providing that? She asks the chickens questions, like Robin Wall Kimmerer did to plants. Or like Vinciane Despret, who wants to get to know birds by turning the perspective around, asking: What does the bird pay attention to? What does it long for?[37] Or: How does it move through the time-space continuum? The bird becomes someone we watch and listen to, but who also watches and listens themselves. Just like Kamphof's chickens, who all become a "somebody." What does it mean to live with such totally different somebodies? How to have a good time together? The relationship between humans and chickens starts to transcend the familiar, like a dream of interspecies understanding and friendship. It's made possible by "tools of curiosity": techniques that physically train perception, both Kamphof's and the chickens'. The attunement, or "bodily resonance" as Kamphof calls it, is mutual.[38]

RESONATING WITH A STONE

Resonance is becoming a popular concept, due in no small part to the work of cultural sociologist Hartmut Rosa, who has put it on the map as a value under pressure in technological times, for example in *The Uncontrollability of the World*.[39] Resonance occurs when you are affected by something external, such as a piece of music, a landscape, or another person. It's a moment of touch. You feel you are being addressed and that you may react, though you can never fully possess that which touches you. It's uncontrollable or unattainable; it will always partly escape your grasp. For instance, you can own an LP or a photograph, but not the music or sunset captured on it.

This would render the practice of recording bird sounds with a smartphone—often against the backdrop of a sunset—pointless and perhaps even reprehensible. It could be seen as an attempt to take control over the uncontrollable. For Rosa, it seems impossible for resonance to be mediated by (digital) technology. But isn't that too strict? I can't control the wind in the trees, and yet making a recording helps me establish a meaningful relationship with the trees and the environment, with myself, and even with something as uncontrollable as beauty.

Rosa rightly points out that acceleration and fragmentation undermine the experience of resonance. Conversely, that means that resonance demands slowing down and concentration, and that means distance from our screens. Chances are, the moment I grab my phone to start a recording, I receive a message that swallows up my attention, taking me away from the bird chorus or tree duet. I would be better off using a professional recorder or camera, preferably without an internet connection. Even then, however, my experience of resonance would be mediated by a technological device, and I would be preoccupied with trying to control the uncontrollable.

To experience resonance, Rosa argues, one must learn to listen carefully. He frequently mentions the importance of paying attention to the appeal that goes out from the world. "This is what mountain climbers mean when they say that every mountain has 'its own character,' and why sailors say that you have to listen closely to the sea to understand it."[40] I suspect that in doing so mountain climbers and sailors to a large extent rely on intuition, that they have developed a kind of third ear for the natural world before them. But they must also rely on technologies to climb and navigate, gauging depth and altitude for them as a kind of extension of their senses, much like a musician whose instrument becomes an extra body part. Their listening must be a superfocused state of perception, as well as a unification with the world, of which technology is a part. It cannot be done without instruments.

Resonance is an encounter of discipline and surrender, a strange paradox in which the active and passive merge. Something external touches you; it happens to you. And then, it evokes an efficacy of the self: the ability to respond and bring something about through your own actions. Resonance requires both touch and response, but being touched by something beyond your control must come first. Just as listening precedes speaking and the trees are present before I hear their rustling.

In addition to self-efficacy, I believe there's also something you could call "self-afficacy": your ability to affect or touch others. The importance of this should not be underestimated. Just as I am the center of my own world, which I share with all sorts of others, creatures, trees, buildings, structures, and systems that interact with me and impact me, so, too, is everyone else. And for them I belong to what's out there, to that which can touch them in an instant, for better or worse.

▶ ▷ ▶

To Rosa, technology is, above all, a burden that blocks resonance. It was invented precisely to make things controllable, efficient, and available. The most far-reaching technology that we have developed to make nature available to us, according to Rosa, is nuclear fission. It's also the most radical example of how the drive for control ultimately leads to its opposite, a loss of control of the most frightening kind, since radiation is "silent, invisible, odorless, impalpable."[41]

This presents another limit to listening. Can you experience resonance with an atom, as I do when I listen to the wind in the trees? This is a serious challenge. Could we develop a "planetary consciousness," as philosopher Achille Mbembe asks, by listening at the level of the very smallest and the very largest?[42] A consciousness that is necessary to build a different relationship with nature? That would require us to try to experience resonance in all areas and by all means, rather than excluding things in advance.

It's hard to imagine how to resonate with an atom. Is it possible to listen to that which not only doesn't speak, but doesn't even seem to produce any sound at all? Something that moves on such a different time-space continuum that you can count on neither efficacy nor "afficacy"? I think so. If the mountain climber can listen to the massiveness of a mountain, why should the smallest particles remain silent? If you can establish a relationship with the ocean, why not with the planet?

Juan Arturo García's film *Time, Displaced* tells an enigmatic story about a nuclear reactor in Colombia, where research is being conducted on the primal sounds of the earth, which are both unimaginably loud and tiny.[43] Can you hear a mountain grow? someone asks. Perhaps you can, is the suggestion, if you try to listen to the "mumbling" of atoms, as happens in nuclear reactors. "All matter sounds all the time at an atomic level simply because it is vibrating. Sounds can be heard in the spin of electrons, in the quanta of atoms and in the structure of molecules," writes Marcel Cobussen.[44] With enough processing and amplification, this rumbling can become audible to the human ear, much like the cosmic background radiation of the Big Bang.

García's film reminds me of a poem by Wisława Szymborska, in which someone tries to have a conversation with a stone. It starts with a knock on the stone's front door and a rather audacious plea:

> "It's only me, let me come in.
> I want to enter your insides,
> have a look around,
> breathe my fill of you."[45]

The rest of the poem gives the account of a failure. The person's knock draws attention to itself, demands entry, as if saying, "Listen to me!" The stone, however, is adamant and urges the visitor to go away. It has no desire to let this uninvited guest in. And despite persistent pleas, access remains closed.

In *Time, Displaced,* someone is also knocking on a stone, as if trying to extract the earth's secrets. There, too, the knocking is in vain. The stone remains indifferent to this human way of communicating or transmitting. The perspective leads in just one direction. Then, the boy picks up an old-fashioned set of clackers, that act as a kind of pendulum. Perhaps these will enable him to descend into the stone's interior and its constituent particles, which also clack, and that have empty spaces stretching out between them.

Szymborska's visitor flatters the stone with the empty halls that make up its interior, but that remain unappreciated if they can't enter, "their beauty in vain, / soundless, not echoing anyone's steps." But the stone holds firm. I understand. This person's pounding shows little empathy. They may consider themselves curious, but it's at most a narcissistic curiosity, which subjects others to their own gratification. The poem ends in an aporia. One last knock and plea is followed by the stone's final answer: "I don't have a door."

I interpret this as: not-knowing is fundamental. But then, it is all the more remarkable that I was nevertheless able to listen to the stone, through Szymborska's poem.

AESTHETIC RELATIONSHIPS

Techniques and technologies mediate our relationship to the world, each in their own ways. In such mediation, not only ethics matter but aesthetics too, the doctrine of beauty and of sensory perception. All examples of good listeners (to nature or otherwise), employ particularly attentive forms of perception, an aesthetics you could call it, whether regarding chickens, the sea, mountains, or a stone. From such observation arises dedication; aesthetics and ethics appear intimately entangled.[46]

It's not surprising when attentive observation develops into a meaningful relationship. To begin with, it trains your sensory discernment. At first, you only hear the uniform noise of the sea or the deafening twittering of the general category of "birds" at sunrise or sunset. Gradually you learn to distinguish details and hear (and see) blackbirds, thrushes, robins, pigeons, wrens, sparrows, finches, great tits, and so on.

Biologist David G. Haskell argues that the senses "bring us great pleasure at the same time that they're orienting us to the important work of *ethical* discernment."[47] To care about a bird, you must recognize it as a "somebody." And that starts with attentive observation. Your attention is like a line you cast outward and that touches another. Now, you are implicated with one another. Haskell continues, "Using aesthetics—well-informed, deeply rooted aesthetics—as a moral guide is something that needs to come back into fashion." Birds, he says, are a prime example. They have long provided us with aesthetic pleasure and are thus a "gateway drug" to a different relationship with nature. (Let that ingenious idea sink in: birds as a gateway drug.) By learning to recognize and appreciate the beauty of birdsong—in short, by perceiving it aesthetically—you also learn to know and appreciate birds on another, ethical level. Why wouldn't that apply to other areas of being as well?

▶ ▷ ▶

I was delighted to discover that the etymology of the Dutch word "waarnemen," meaning "to perceive," refers back to "paying attention to, caring for." "Waar" means care or attentiveness, in the sense of wanting to protect or guard. The more general meaning of "to observe" or "to notice with your senses" is what remains in the dictionary (next to temporarily taking over someone's tasks or position). This rich etymology indicates a connection between hearing or seeing something and taking care of it. At its core, perceiving is a matter of attention, which has to do with concentration as well as care. Aren't all the different listening techniques I've come across in fact techniques for perceiving through paying attention? And thus, techniques for caring, not by simply agreeing, but rather by staying open before making judgments—and so, ultimately, for *being able to judge with care*?

This brings me back to the complicated notion around which so much of the tech industry revolves. One could argue that online attention is about perception; what counts are the literal numbers of eyeballs that have encountered something. But that throws perception and attention onto the same quantified pile, with care as exiled excess on the road to profit.

Aesthetic discernment—which is also ethical discernment—is indispensable because perception can easily be fooled in an era of deep fakes, AI, and other manipulations. That makes being attentive all the more urgent. Not so much through questioning whether something is real or not but rather in considering how different techniques shape our perception and what their implications are. How aesthetic discernment can be trained, in order to move towards ethical relationships. From the self to the other. And finally, from listening to speaking.

INTERIORITY AND TOGETHERNESS

Even if it is foggy or noisy in there, interiority should be the starting point. Although tech companies like to deny its existence, even a short listening exercise lets you hear its echo. In her journal, Marion Milner describes how she listens not only to music but also to her own thoughts. She discovers there are two Marions: her conscious self and a voice that answers when she lets her thoughts run their course. She resolves to investigate that second voice more closely, including through automatic writing.

It's not a surprise if a psychoanalyst discovers that her automatic voice—which could be called the voice of the subconscious—speaks from childhood fears, full of negativity and uncertainty, casting an irrational shadow over her adult existence. This seems to explain why she has so much trouble making life decisions; she is ruled by two conflicting selves. However, this realization alone is enough to settle the battle. She writes, "It puzzled me that these back-of-my-mind thoughts should have such power to spread an emotional shadow. Time and again I would find one of them filling me with gloomy forebodings and yet, when I had caught it and turned my searchlight upon it, it was but a little thing, a trivial difficulty which I knew quite well how to surmount."[48] This sounds like Milner possesses an extraordinarily tidy mind, despite those two selves. A few childhood voices wail through but those can easily be defused—not everyone will recognize themselves in that.

Nevertheless, it's healthy to listen to your subconscious with the intention of getting to know what you hear, rather than wanting to express it directly. Which doesn't mean you shouldn't express yourself; it mainly indicates that the automatic thoughts that bubble up are usually not the most helpful, insightful, pleasant, or desired ones. Or the most true or real, either. Too often, automatism is confused with authenticity.

Apart from this tangle of voices that must be tamed with persistence and rationality, the inner self must remain obscure and impenetrable, a thing as unknowable as anything else around you. We have that in common with the stone. You might say the stone has no inner being; its outside is its inside. Yet that stone too has an existence and a history, and you can approach it as a someone. It has a perspective, at least aesthetically speaking. You can establish a reciprocal relationship with it. It may start with you, but it doesn't have to end there.

▶ ▷ ▶

That reminds me of another one of Virginia Woolf's novels, *The Waves.* A chorus of different voices tells the story of six, seven friends. Or maybe it's a chain rather than a chorus. The individual voices, lives, and bodies remain distinct, alternating in their oral testimonies. A shared chain of witnessing unfolds, a collective perception, moreover, one that is embedded within a planetary consciousness.

Woolf captures that planetary stream of consciousness in passages featuring trees, birds and, of course, waves; scenes of night and day and back to night, of sunrise, zenith, and sunset, darkness and light, energy and lethargy, and death. How the birds "swept and soared sharply inflights high into the air, twittering short, sharp notes . . . . Now and again their songs ran together in swift scales like the interlacings of a mountain stream whose waters, meeting, foam and then mix, and hasten quicker and quicker down the same channel, brushing the same broad leaves. But there is a rock; they sever."[49]

I was about to disappear in the stream of sounds, but then. "Listen: a whistle sounds, wheels rush, the door creaks on its hinges." I turn my head, hear the noises move around me. "I regain the sense of the complexity and the reality and the struggle, for which I thank you." I turn another quarter to face the other. "And with some pity, some envy and much good will, take your hand and bid you good night."[50]

I know I can't stay quiet, not forever.

I nod, I say, "Goodbye."

Epilogue

The Ethics of Listening

If you already know what you want to hear and are looking for confirmation, or if you're waiting for your turn to speak, then you're probably not listening. But just like much speaking is aimed at taking a position—though not all speaking is—so, too, is much listening aimed at encapsulating what is heard—though not all listening. Not what I now must label "good listening."

Listening—the attentive perception of an auditory source of information that in many cases is fleeting, invisible, and unrepeatable—is at best a movement toward knowing. It starts from the unknown and inevitably returns or ends there. Listening—open and sensory listening—relates to the here and now, to myself and the specific person or other being who is with me, and is thus primarily a lesson in dealing with the unknown. The unknown out there, and in here. Perhaps that's why many people do not venture into it. The unknown isn't necessarily pleasant or even interesting. Sometimes it's painful or dangerous. And because the unknown also rests within the self, all of that is equally true there.

Yet I think it also brings something welcome. A certain calmness. Steadfastness. If you are aware of the unknown in yourself, you don't have to let every external blow shake you. Others can do as they wish; making it about me isn't obligatory. This is also useful for when you encounter the limit of what you want to hear. Instead of defending or entrenching yourself, it creates space for further inquiry. Even unwelcome things are worthy of attention, if only to recognize them more quickly next time.

In the words of the transmission model, listening is not just receiving but also sending. After all, paying attention is an active process. An attentive listener isn't just out to get something, for example, like knowledge. First of all, they want to give something.

This gift interests me. What exactly is being given away here? It sounds like something precious. However, what the listener is gifting is nothingness, a purposelessness that is open and free. Still, this gift of nothingness strikes me as heavy-handed. Perhaps because it's accompanied by trust. Of course, trust can be violated again and again. But isn't that also why it is so valuable? You relinquish control and place it in the hands of another. Giving also means: handing over. Who can untangle sending and receiving now?

"Attention is the rarest and purest form of generosity," said Simone Weil, offering a quote that is Instagram-worthy on several levels.[1] Attention and generosity are connected through giving. In this day and age, generosity sounds like a virtue reserved for the wealthy and an unjust demand on those who cannot afford it. But it isn't. Listening is generous, and free. You've never earned the nothingness you give away, and nor can you lose it. It is an inexhaustible abundance. The pure act of generosity, writes Buddhist author Taitetsu Unno, has "no giver, no gift, and no receiver."[2] No model and no transmission.

▶ ▷ ▶

In the work of anthropologist David Scott, I read about the concept of "receptive generosity."[3] A generous person is traditionally seen as someone who gives without expecting anything in return. They need nothing for themselves; they are sovereign individuals who never lacked anything. But such self-sufficiency disguised as generosity, though it may seem virtuous, can also be arrogant. Giving something to others without any reciprocity can also be a way to gain or maintain control. It's the expression of a monological relationship. Receptive generosity, on the other hand, is a two-way street.

Being a good recipient isn't easy. It implies wanting or needing something that you cannot get on your own. It requires you to be open to what comes your way, which entails a certain vulnerability, according to Scott. He concludes, "Receptivity . . . is the side of generosity that is harder to cultivate. Paradoxically, receiving is more difficult than giving."[4] The same can be said about the attention technique that is listening, which is more difficult than speaking. Moreover, in a dialogic ethic, everyone is both sender and receiver at the same time. In that case, someone who knows how to give but not how to receive misses out on everything.

▶ ▷ ▶

In a context dominated by data, profit, shareholders, and power, could there be receptive and generous technology?

Can we give space to dialogical ethics when we are trapped in a system that hardly encourages it and even actively opposes it?

"The" technology does not exist. Even the dominant structures that shape our communication are merely one manifestation of it, though they can never be fully reversed or eliminated. It helps to understand technology as a well-defined yet accidental set of techniques that mediate our being in the world and shape the relationships we form and maintain, on both the sending and receiving ends.

In addition to social media, algorithms, recommendations, chat apps, chatbots, group apps, reply-all emails, reply-guys, fake news websites, satirical news blogs, show news, news shows, game shows, talk shows, columns, commentaries, and conspiracy channels there sounds a chorus, a chime, an orchestra of techniques, which, in the end, trace the known back to the unknown, don't disdain knowledge but call for the relativization of truth and ego, for the willingness to be touched and the realization that you touch others yourself. To begin with oneself but not ending there; to start from oneself but not to aim at it; to be oneself but not remain that way.

"Attention! Attention!" it sounds. It is no other call than: Listen! What do you hear now, and now? And now, fifteen minutes later?

Acknowledgments

A very last exercise in listening. Everyone stands in a circle. One person says their name, the group repeats it. Then the next name sounds and is repeated in chorus.

These voices echo throughout this book: Aldo, Anneroos, Ariel, Arjen, Arthur, Ayse, Bart, Bas, Blair, Brendan, Caspar, Christine, Coen, Costica, Cris, Dirk, Dirk, Elisabet, Els, Emma, Emy, Esther, Femke, Femke, Fiep, Geert, Geertje, Göran, GT, Hans, Hans, Herman, Hester, Inge, Jan, Jeroen, Jessica, Julia, Justin, Karin, Lotfi, Lozzi, Maarten, Macarena, Marianne, Marijke, Mariska, Marjan, Marlous, Martina, Martine, Mathijn, Mathijs, Matthijs, Melle, Merlijn, Michel, Michelle, Miriam, Miriyam, Mirjam, Nadine, Nikki, Nirav, Onno, Paul, Pim, Rachida, Remco, Rens, Roger, Rogier, Saskia, Senka, Sjors, Sonia, Stephan, Taco Hidde, Tamara, Tanny, Tetiana, Timo, Tonnie, Veerle, Vivian, Willem, Willemien.

A huge thank you goes out to everyone who made possible my stay at the Netherlands Institute for Advanced Study in the Humanities and Social Sciences, all the lovely and hardworking people at Columbia University Press and at my Dutch publisher De Bezige Bij, Costica Bradatan for his unbounded trust in the project from the very start, plus the anonymous reviewers. This book wouldn't have existed without you.

Notes

Translations of all Dutch sources are by the author

Prologue

1. Lundahl & Seitl, *Infinite Conversations*, April 9, 2022, participatory performance, STRP Festival, Eindhoven. *The Infinite Conversation* is a seminal work by Maurice Blanchot, trans. Susan Hanson (University of Minnesota Press, 1993).
2. Simone Weil, *Waiting for God*, trans. Emma Craufurd (Harper Perennial, 1973), 111.
3. Dominic Burbidge and Andrew Briggs, *Citizenship in a Networked Age: An Agenda for Rebuilding Our Civic Ideals* (University of Oxford, 2020), 9. Listening skills are added to different higher educational or vocational training programs, such as medical and social work education. In *The Empathy Exams* (Graywolf Press, 2014), Leslie Jamison gives an insider's perspective into such trainings for medical students.
4. Burbidge and Briggs, *Citizenship in a Networked Age*, 168.
5. Hans Jonas, "The Nobility of Sight: A Study in the Phenomenology of the Senses," *Philosophy and Phenomenological Research* 14, no. 4 (June 1954): 517.

6. Jean-Luc Nancy, *Listening*, trans. Charlotte Mandell (Fordham University Press, 2007).
7. Rolando Vázquez Melken, "Towards a Decolonial Critique of Modernity: *Buen Vivir*, Relationality and the Task of Listening," in *Capital, Poverty, Development*, ed. Raúl Fornet-Betancourt (Wissenschaftsverlag Mainz, 2012), 248.
8. Rolando Vázquez Melken, *Vistas of Modernity: Decolonial Aesthesis and the End of the Contemporary* (Mondrian Fund, 2020), 156–157.

1. The Context of Technology

1. Ineke van der Hurk, host, *In het hoofd van*, podcast, season 1, episode 1, "Wat als paniekaanvallen je constant achtervolgen?,"NPO Luister/HUMAN, June 6, 2023, https://npo.nl/luister/podcasts/920-in-het-hoofd-van/91178.

2. Marshall McLuhan, *Understanding Media: The Extensions of Man* (MIT Press, 1994).
3. R. Murray Schafer, *The Soundscape: Our Sonic Environment and the Tuning of the World* (Destiny Books, 1994), 11.
4. "Het nieuwe luisteren," FD Media Group, November 23, 2022, https://fdmg.nl/nieuws/het-nieuwe-luisteren-nieuw-publiek-en-nieuwe-kansen/.
5. Mina Etemad, "Podcastkritiek: 'Mag ik bij jullie aanschuiven?,'" accessed February 27, 2026, https://podcastfestival.nl/podcastkritiek-mag-ik-bij-jullie-aanschuiven/.
6. Roel Griffioen, Salomé Voegelin, and Sjoerd Leijten, hosts, *Radical Murmur*, podcast, season 1, episode 1, "The Sonic City," TRASHLINIE, October 17, 2022, https://trashlinie.org/.
7. Veronica Esposito, "The Upside of Being an Avatar: Critical Communities on the Web," in *The Digital Critic: Literary Culture Online*, ed. Houman Barekat, Robert Barry, and David Winters (OR Books, 2017), EPUB.
8. Stefanie Gordin, "'Social media justice warriors" bereiken een nieuwe generatie stemmers," *One World*, August 22, 2023, www.oneworld.nl/mensenrechten/deze-social-media-justice-warriors-bereiken-een-nieuwe-generatie-stemmers/.

9. Kwago, *Oyayi,* April 13–16, 2023, installation, STRP Festival, Eindhoven.
10. bell hooks, *Teaching to Transgress: Education as the Practice of Freedom* (Routledge, 1994), 40.
11. Peter-Paul Verbeek, "Beyond Interaction: A Short Introduction to Mediation Theory," *Interactions* 22, no. 3 (May–June 2015): 26–31.
12. Pauline Oliveros, *Quantum Listening* (Ignota Books, 2022), 30.
13. Jaron Harambam and Marije Kuiper, *The Truth Is Out There* (Volt, 2021).
14. Robert Pfaller, *Interpassivity: The Aesthetics of Delegated Enjoyment* (Edinburgh University Press, 2017).
15. Byung-Chul Han, "The Information Regime," in *Infocracy: Digitization and the Crisis of Democracy*, trans. Daniel Steuer (Polity Press, 2022), EPUB.
16. Han, "Infocracy," in *Infocracy*.
17. Han.
18. Marshall McLuhan, *The Gutenberg Galaxy: The Making of Typographic Man* (University of Toronto Press, 1962).
19. Georg Simmel, "The Metropolis and Mental Life," in *On Individuality and Social Forms: Selected Writings*, ed. Donald N. Levine (University of Chicago Press, 1971), 324–339.
20. Mack Hagood, *Hush: Media and Sonic Self-Control* (Duke University Press, 2019), 4.
21. Hagood, *Hush*, 4.
22. Hagood.
23. Gijs Beukers, "Luister dan!—We luisteren steeds slechter, maar gelukkig kunnen we het leren," *de Volkskrant*, May 12, 2020; Kate Murphy, *You're Not Listening: What You're Missing and Why It Matters* (Celadon Books, 2019), EPUB.
24. Peter Pomerantsev, *This is Not Propaganda: Adventures in the War Against Reality* (Faber & Faber, 2019), "Part 4: Soft Facts," EPUB.
25. Estelle Frankel, *The Wisdom of Not-Knowing: Discovering a Life of Wonder by Embracing Uncertainty* (Shambhala Publications, 2017), 163.
26. Ted Chiang, "The Great Silence," Electric Literature, October 12, 2016, https://electricliterature.com/the-great-silence-by-ted-chiang/.
27. Zeno Siemens-Brega and Jacco Prantl, "Jij dacht dat je goed kon luisteren? Luister dan eens naar deze man met microfoon," *De Correspondent*, June 13, 2020, https://decorrespondent.nl/11305/jij-dacht

-dat-je-goed-kon-luisteren-luister-dan-eens-naar-deze-man-met-microfoon/0af8153b-abad-0646-3c0c-7cc96720a075.

28. Lisbeth Lipari, *Listening, Thinking, Being: Toward an Ethics of Attunement* (Pennsylvania State University Press, 2014), 10.
29. Lipari, *Listening, Thinking, Being,* 111.
30. Lipari, 126.
31. Raviv Ganchrow, "Earth-Bound Sound: Oscillations of Hearing, Ocean, and Air," *Theory & Event* 24, no. 1 (January 2021): 68–69.
32. Lawrence Abu Hamdan, "Forensic Listening as Machine Listening: Lawrence Abu Hamdan in Conversation with James Parker," *Disclaimer,* September 13, 2020, https://disclaimer.org.au/contents/forensic-listening-as-machine-listening.
33. Joseph Turow, *The Voice Catchers: How Marketers Listen In to Exploit Your Feelings, Your Privacy, and Your Wallet* (Yale University Press, 2021).
34. Thao Phan, "Machine Listening: Thao Phan: Listening to Misrecognition," Liquid Architecture, YouTube, January 18, 2022, 1 hr., 19 min., 3 sec., www.youtube.com/watch?v=D3vbd4QHebo&t=2388s.
35. Florian Henckel von Donnersmarck, dir., *Das Leben der Anderen* (Buena Vista International, 2006).
36. "Machine Listening," accessed February 27, 2026, https://machinelistening.exposed/.
37. Abu Hamdan, "Forensic Listening as Machine Listening."
38. Joeri Bruyninckx, "Luistervinken," *Wijsgerig perspectief* 62, no. 3 (2022): 31.
39. Bruyninckx, "Luistervinken," 31. Literally: "spread out listening."
40. Bruyninckx.
41. See, e.g., Vinciane Despret, *Living as a Bird,* trans. Helen Morrison (Polity Press, 2021).
42. Turow, *Voice Catchers,* 6.
43. Marjolein Voogel, "Lezen of je leven ervan afhangt," *de Nederlandse Boekengids,* no. 5 (2022), www.nederlandseboekengids.com/20220915-marjolijn-voogel/.

2. The Wish for Dialogue

1. Jim Jarmusch, dir., *Paterson* (Amazon Studios, Bleeker Street, Le Pacte, and K5 International, 2016).

2. Özlem Cekic, "Why I Have Coffee with People Who Send Me Hate Mail," TED, September 2018, 15 min., 11 sec., www.ted.com/talks/ozlem_cekic_why_i_have_coffee_with_people_who_send_me_hate_mail.
3. Paulius Senūta, "The Battle Against Fake News" (Conference panel, Public Spaces Conference, Amsterdam, May 17, 2022), https://conference.publicspaces.net/en/session/he-1. The original website, callrussia.org, has been offline since the end of 2025.
4. Michael Sandel, "Culture Wars and the Myth of the Neutral State," *Noema*, April 14, 2026, https://www.noemamag.com/the-vulnerability-of-the-liberal-neutral-state/.
5. Liesbeth Levy, *Dialoog, meer dan een pacificatie-instrument. Lessen uit Rotterdam* (Trichis, 2020).
6. Bart Brandsma, *Polarisatie. Inzicht in de dynamiek van wij-zij denken* (n.p., 2016).
7. David Bohm, *On Dialogue* (Taylor and Francis, 2004), 14.
8. Bohm, *On Dialogue*, 2.
9. Carl R. Rogers and Richard E. Farson, "Active Listening," in *Communicating in Business Today*, ed. R. G. Newman, M. A. Danzinger, and M. Cohen (D.C. Heath, 1987), 592.
10. Marlou van Paridon, *Socratisch gesprek voor beginners. Een praktisch handboek* (ISVW Uitgevers, 2017); Marc van Dijk, "Kristof Van Rossem: Leeg luisteren kun je leren," *Filosofie Magazine*, September 22, 2023, www.filosofie.nl/kristof-van-rossem-leeg-luisteren-kun-je-leren/.
11. Dan Lyons, *STFU: The Power of Keeping Your Mouth Shut in an Endlessly Noisy World* (Henry Holt, 2023), 1.
12. Erika James and Lynn Perry Wooten, "In a Crisis, Great Leaders Prioritize Listening," *Harvard Business Review*, September 13, 2022, https://hbr.org/2022/09/in-a-crisis-great-leaders-prioritize-listening.
13. Guy Itzchakov and Avraham N. (Avi) Kluger, "The Power of Listening in Helping People Change," *Harvard Business Review*, May 17, 2018, https://hbr.org/2018/05/the-power-of-listening-in-helping-people-change.
14. Glen Llopis, "6 Ways Effective Listening Can Make You a Better Leader," *Forbes*, May 20, 2103, www.forbes.com/sites/glennllopis/2013/05/20/6-effective-ways-listening-can-make-you-a-better-leader/.

2. THE WISH FOR DIALOGUE

15. Kate Murphy, *You're Not Listening: What You're Missing and Why It Matters* (Celadon Books, 2019), "5. The Tone-Deaf Response: Why People Would Rather Talk to Their Dog," EPUB.
16. Simone Weil, *Waiting for God*, trans. Emma Craufurd (Harper Perennial, 1973), 111.
17. Krista Ratcliffe, "Rhetorical Listening: A Trope for Interpretive Invention and a 'Code of Cross-Cultural Conduct,'" *College Composition and Communication* 51, no. 2 (December 1999): 203.
18. Ratcliffe, "Rhetorical Listening," 203.
19. Tripta Chandola, *Listening into Others: An Ethnographic Exploration in Govindpuri* (Institute of Network Cultures, 2020).
20. Chandola, *Listening into Others*, 58.
21. Chandola, 95.
22. Chandola, 19.
23. Pauline Oliveros, *Quantum Listening* (Ignota Books, 2022), 30.
24. See, e.g., Emmanuel Levinas, *Totality and Infinity: An Essay on Exteriority*, trans. Alphonso Lingis (Duquesne University Press, 1969).
25. Lisbeth Lipari, *Listening, Thinking, Being: Toward an Ethics of Attunement* (Pennsylvania State University Press, 2014), 195.
26. Emmanuel Levinas, *Ethics and Infinity: Conversations with Philippe Nemo*, trans. Richard A. Cohen (Duquesne University Press, 1985), 89.
27. Emmanuel Levinas, *Otherwise Than Being or Beyond Essence*, trans. Alphonso Lingis (Kluwer Academic Publishers, 1991), 6.
28. Lipari, *Listening, Thinking, Being*, 175–204.
29. Byung-Chul Han, *Psychopolitics: Neoliberalism and New Technologies of Power*, trans. Erik Butler (Verso, 2017), "13. Idiotism," EPUB.
30. Martin Buber, *The Way of Man According to the Teachings of Hasidism* (Wilcox & Follett, 1951), 35.
31. Arthur Rimbaud, "Lettre de Rimbaud à Paul Demeny—15 mai 1871," Wikisource, last modified February 27, 2026, https://fr.wikisource.org/wiki/Lettre_de_Rimbaud_%C3%A0_Paul_Demeny_-_15_mai_1871.
32. Mikhail Bakhtin, "Discourse in the Novel," in *The Dialogic Imagination*, trans. Caryl Emerson and Michael Holquist (University of Texas Press, 2008), 293–294.
33. Mikhail Bakhtin, *Problems of Dostoevsky's Poetics*, trans. Caryl Emerson (University of Minnesota Press, 1984), 82.

34. Anton Simons, *Het groteske van de taal. Over het werk van Michail Bachtin* (SUA, 1990), 107.
35. Building Conversation, *Distant Thoughts*, June 2, 2021, participatory performance from home, STRP Festival.
36. Marja Pruis, "Iemand nog wat drinken?," *De Groene Amsterdammer*, July 30, 2014.
37. M. M. Bakhtin, *Art and Answerability*, ed. Michael Holquist and Vadim Liapunov, trans. Vadim Liapunov (University of Texas Press, 1990), 89.
38. Simons, *Het groteske van de taal*, 84.
39. Keith Kahn-Harris, "The Pleasure in Not Understanding a Language Can Be Awesome," *Psyche*, January 19, 2022, https://psyche.co/ideas/the-pleasure-in-not-understanding-a-language-can-be-awesome.
40. Lipari, *Listening, Thinking, Being*, 140.
41. An interesting parallel can be drawn with the value of "misreading" for literature, as explained by Harold Bloom in his book *A Map of Misreading* (Oxford University Press, 2003). Thank you to one of the reviewers for this suggestion.
42. Bob Chisholm and Jeff Harrison, "Introduction," in *The Wisdom of Not-Knowing: Essays on Psychotherapy, Buddhism, and Life Experience*, ed., Bob Chisholm and Jeff Harrison (Triarchy Press, 2016), 7.
43. Estelle Frankel, *The Wisdom of Not-Knowing: Discovering a Life of Wonder by Embracing Uncertainty* (Shambhala Publications, 2017), 170.
44. Perhaps even being of spiritual descent, echoing the notion of "spiritual acoustics" that speaks from the work of Søren Kierkegaard; see Kevin Hart, *Kierkegaard and Phenomenology* (Cambridge University Press, 2025), 36–51.

3. The Tradition of Testimony

1. Valeria Luiselli, *Tell Me How It Ends: An Essay in Forty Questions* (4th Estate, 2017), EPUB.
2. Luiselli, *Tell Me How It Ends*, "1. Border," EPUB.
3. Valeria Luiselli, *Lost Children Archive* (Knopf, 2019), EPUB.
4. Luiselli, *Lost Children Archive*, "Undocumented," EPUB.
5. Paul Celan, "Aschenglorie," cited in Rachel Zolf, *No One's Witness: A Monstrous Poetics* (Duke University Press, 2021), 130–131.

6. "Saddam Hussein," Wikipedia, last modified February 27, 2026, https://en.wikipedia.org/wiki/Saddam_Hussein.
7. Bernie Glassman, *Bearing Witness: A Zen Master's Lessons in Making Peace* (Bell Tower, 1999), 78.
8. See, e.g., Annelie Pohlen, "Armando," *Art Forum* 23, no. 9 (May 1985), www.artforum.com/events/armando-2-224407/.
9. Shoshana Felman and Dori Laub, *Testimony: Crises of Witnessing in Literature, Psychoanalysis, and History* (Routledge, 1992).
10. Felman and Laub, *Testimony*, 75.
11. Giorgio Agamben, *Remnants of Auschwitz: The Witness and the Archive*, trans. Daniel Heller-Roazen (Zone Books, 2002), 17.
12. Susan Sontag, *Regarding the Pain of Others* (Farrar, Straus and Giroux, 2003).
13. Sontag, *Regarding the Pain of Others*, 66.
14. Sontag, 72.
15. Arne De Winde, "Sterven op de smartphone: In gesprek met Mareike Meis," *Rekto:Verso*, August 31, 2022, www.rektoverso.be/artikel/sterven-op-de-smartphone-in-gesprek-met-mareike-meis.
16. Nadia de Vries, "Digital Corpses: Creation, Appropriation, and Reappropriation" (PhD diss., University of Amsterdam, 2020), 12.
17. Sontag, *Regarding the Pain of Others*, 101.
18. Cited in Lisa Weeda, "Hoe kun je fictie schrijven over een oorlog die nog niet voorbij is?," *ILFU*, June 12, 2022, https://ilfu.com/alle-artikelen/lisa-weeda-over-andrej-koerkov.
19. Cited in Tobias Waltz, "Oekraïense schrijvers en de oorlog: waarom de woorden nog niet komen," *NRC Handelsblad*, February 24, 2023.
20. Eva Peek, "Oekraïense dichteres Natalka Bilotserkivets: 'Hoe kan iemand nu nadenken over de schoonheid van poëzie?,' " *NRC Handelsblad*, June 9, 2023.
21. Tetiana Belimova, "Wording of Trauma, Recording Memory," *Eurozine*, November 13, 2023, www.eurozine.com/wording-of-trauma-recording-memory/.
22. Janita Monna, "Oekraïens-Amerikaanse dichter Ilya Kaminsky: Poëzie doet ertoe, dus bewaar dichtregels op een veilige plek," *Trouw*, April 28, 2023.
23. Toef Jaeger, "Dove Oekraïense dichter Ilya Kaminsky: 'Stilte is een uitvinding van de horenden,' " *NRC Handelsblad*, June 8, 2022.

24. Ilya Kaminsky, *Deaf Republic* (Graywolf Press, 2019), "In a Time of Peace," EPUB.
25. Felman and Laub, *Testimony*, 70.
26. Felman and Laub, 58.
27. Felman and Laub, 57.
28. Svetlana Alexievich, *In Search of The Free Individual: The History of the Russian-Soviet Soul*, trans. Jamey Gambrell (Cornell University Press, 2018), 11.
29. Svetlana Alexievich, *The Unwomanly Face of War*, trans. Larissa Volokhonsky and Richard Pevear (Random House, 2018), xviii.
30. Svetlana Alexievich and Staffan Julén, dirs., *Lyubov: Love in Russia* (Taskovski Films, 2017).
31. Miranda Fricker, *Epistemic Injustice: Power and the Ethics of Knowing* (Oxford University Press, 2007), 9–29.
32. Sarah Polley, dir., *Women Talking* (United Artists Releasing, 2022).
33. Emma Cooper, dir., *Depp v Heard*, a three-part series aired on Chanel 4 in the United Kingdom on May 21, 2023, and released internationally on Netflix.
34. Agamben, *Remnants of Auschwitz*, 18.
35. Jacques Derrida, "'A Self-Unsealing Poetic Text': Poetics and Politics of Witnessing," trans. Rachel Bowlby, in *Revenge of the Aesthetic: The Place of Literature in Theory Today*, ed. Michael P. Clark (University of California Press, 2010), 180–207.
36. Anneleen Spiessens, "Getuigenis in vertaling: Inleiding," *Filter* 1 (2018), http://hdl.handle.net/1854/LU-8571272.
37. Marloes Geboers and Esther Hammelburg, "Doe niet mee aan de mediaoorlog," *Het Parool*, October 20, 2023.
38. Wendy H. K. Chun, "Unbearable Witness: Toward a Politics of Listening," *Differences: A Journal of Feminist Cultural Studies* 11, no. 1 (1999): 112–149.
39. Odile Heynders, "The Critical Pedagogy of Fiction in Democratic Public Spheres," in *Authorship, Activism and Celebrity: Art and Action in Global Literature*, ed. Sandra Mayer and Ruth Scobie (Bloomsbury, 2023), 111–124.
40. Peter Pomerantsev and Joanna Kavenna, "In Conversation," *Granta*, August 5, 2019, https://granta.com/joanna-kavenna-and-peter-pomerantsev-in-conversation/.

3. THE TRADITION OF TESTIMONY

41. Maggie Nelson, *The Art of Cruelty: A Reckoning* (Norton, 2011), 130.
42. Susan Schuppli, *Material Witness* (MIT Press, 2020).
43. Thao Phan, "Machine Listening: Thao Phan: Listening to Misrecognition," Liquid Architecture, YouTube, January 18, 2022, 1 hr., 19 min., 3 sec., www.youtube.com/watch?v=D3vbd4QHebo&t=2388s.
44. Lawrence Abu Hamdan, "Forensic Listening as Machine Listening: Lawrence Abu Hamdan in Conversation with James Parker," *Disclaimer*, September 13, 2020, https://disclaimer.org.au/contents/forensic-listening-as-machine-listening.
45. Atef Abu Saif, *The Drone Eats with Me: A Gaza Diary* (Beacon Press, 2016), 4.
46. Abu Saif, *Drone Eats with Me*, 21.
47. Abu Saif, 31.
48. "Earwitness Inventory, 2018–Ongoing," Lawrence Abu Hamdan, accessed February 27, 2026, http://lawrenceabuhamdan.com/earwitness-inventory.
49. "Earwitness Inventory."

4. Listening Practice

1. Pan Daijing, musical performance, November 5, 2022, FAQ Festival, Den Bosch.
2. Marion Milner, *A Life of One's Own* (Routledge, 2011), 23.
3. Huba De Graaff, musical performance, April 7, 2023, Het Concreet, Tilburg.
4. David Toop, *Sinister Resonance: The Mediumship of the Listener* (A&C Black, 2010).
5. Toop, *Sinister Resonance*, 75.
6. Piet Mondrian, *Victory Boogie Woogie*, 1942–1944, oil, tape, paper, charcoal and pencil on canvas, 178.4 cm × 178.4 cm, Kunstmuseum Den Haag.
7. Virginia Woolf, *Jacob's Room* (Project Gutenberg E-Book, 2004), chapter 3, EPUB.
8. Pauline Oliveros, *Quantum Listening* (Ignota Books, 2022), 33.
9. *Homing Inside Out: A Listening Guide for Home Quarantine* (Soundtrackcity, 2020), 11 and 4. A 14-pg. PDF download.

10. "#StayHomeSounds," Cities and Memory, https://citiesandmemory.com/covid19-sounds/.
11. Elise 't Hart, "Symfonie voor Huisgeluid, 2022," instituut voor huisgeluid, projecten, accessed February 28, 2026, https://www.instituutvoorhuisgeluid.nl/projecten#symfonie-voor-huisgeluid.
12. Marcel Cobussen, *Engaging with Everyday Sounds* (Open Book Publishers, 2022), 61.
13. Roel Griffioen and Sjoerd Leijten, hosts, *Radical Murmur*, podcast, season 1, episode 3, "Reflections Amidst the Noise," TRASHLINIE, October 17, 2022, https://trashlinie.org/.
14. Haytham El-Wardany, *How to Disappear*, trans. Jennifer Peterson and Robin Moger (Kayfa ta, 2013), 15.
15. Virginia Woolf, *Between the Acts* (Penguin, 2000), EPUB.
16. Pauline Oliveros, *Deep Listening: A Composer's Sound Practice* (Deep Listening Publications, 2005), 13.
17. "Listening as a Compositional Tool," workshop at Het Concreet, Tilburg, April 7, 2023.
18. See Oliveros, *Quantum Listening*, 14.
19. Mastodon account "sounddescription," accessed February 28, 2026, https://uff.rip/about.
20. Evelyn Glennie, "Hearing Essay," January 1, 2015, www.evelyn.co.uk/hearing-essay/.
21. Oliveros, *Deep Listening*, 20.
22. Oliveros, *Quantum Listening*, 42.
23. Anna Lowenhaupt Tsing, *The Mushroom at the End of the World* (Princeton University Press, 2015), vii.
24. Rachel Carson, *Silent Spring* (Mariner Books, 2002).
25. Robin Wall Kimmerer, *Braiding Sweetgrass: Indigenous Wisdom, Scientific Knowledge* (Milkweed Editions, 2013), 346. See also the work of Karen Bakker, *The Sounds of Life: How Digital Technology Is Bringing Us Closer to the Worlds of Animals and Plants* (Princeton University Press, 2022). Thank you to one of the reviewers for this suggestion.
26. Kimmerer, *Braiding Sweetgrass*, 42.
27. Tsing, *Mushroom at the End of the World*, 23.
28. "Embassy of the North Sea," accessed February 28, 2026, www.ambassadevandenoordzee.nl/.

4. LISTENING PRACTICE

29. Bernie Krause, "The Voice of the Natural World," TED, June 2013, 14 min., 34 sec., www.ted.com/talks/bernie_krause_the_voice_of_the_natural_world.
30. Arita Baaijens, *Taal voor de toekomst*, project report, 2021, https://www.taalvoordetoekomst.nl/wp-content/uploads/2022/04/PROJECTVERSLAG_Taalvoordetoekomst_2021_lowres-gecomprimeerd.pdf.
31. Zeno van den Broek and Robin Koek, *Raumklang*, April 13–16, 2023, spatial installation, STRP Festival, Eindhoven.
32. Cherry Duijns, dir., *Toonmeesters*, season 1, episode 1, "Olivier Messiaen," (VPRO, 2013). Also freely available as follows: "Olivier Messiaen, Reinbert de Leeuw - Toonmeesters - Part 2," uploaded by ruurb, YouTube, January 31, 2023, 25 min., 45 sec., https://www.youtube.com/watch?v=X_zGWw96CrI.
33. René van Peer, "Olivier Nijs en Hans Slabbekoorn: Geluiden van mensen in wereld van dieren," *Gonzo (circus)*, no. 166 (November–December 2021), 31–33.

34. Ike Kamphof, "Gereedschap voor nieuwsgierigheid. Over lichamelijke resonantie tussen mens en kip," *Wijsgerig Perspectief* 57, no. 1 (January 2017): 36.
35. Kamphof, "Gereedschap voor nieuwsgierigheid," 38.
36. Kamphof, 39.
37. Vinciane Despret, *Living as a Bird*, trans. Helen Morrison (Polity Press, 2021), 109.
38. Kamphof, "Gereedschap voor nieuwsgierigheid," 41.
39. Hartmut Rosa, *The Uncontrollability of the World*, trans. James C. Wagner (Polity Press, 2020).
40. Rosa, *Uncontrollability of the World*, 48.
41. Rosa, *Uncontrollability of the World*, 116.
42. Achille Mbembe, "How to Develop a Planetary Consciousness," *Noema*, January 11, 2022, www.noemamag.com/how-to-develop-a-planetary-consciousness/.
43. Juan Arturo García, dir., *Time, Displaced*, single-screen video, 20 min. (2023).
44. Cobussen, *Engaging with Everyday Sounds*, 26.
45. Wisława Szymborska, "Conversation with a Stone," in *Poems New and Collected, 1957–1997*, trans. Stanislaw Baranczak and Clare Cavanagh (Harper Collins, 2000).

46. See also Alva Noë, *The Entanglement* (Princeton University Press, 2023).
47. David G. Haskell, "Listening and the Crisis of Inattention," interview by Emmanuel Vaughan-Lee, *Emergence Magazine*, April 21, 2022, https://emergencemagazine.org/interview/listening-and-the-crisis-of-inattention/ (emphasis added).
48. Milner, *Life of One's Own*, 110.
49. Virginia Woolf, *The Waves* (Vintage Classics, 2000), 77.
50. Woolf, *Waves*, 212.

Epilogue: The Ethics of Listening

1. Simone Weil, letter to Joë Bousquet, cited in Simone Pétrement, *Simone Weil: A Life*, trans. Raymond Rosenthal (Pantheon Books, 1976), 462.
2. Taitetsu Unno, *River of Fire, River of Water: An Introduction to the Pure Land Tradition of Shin Buddhism* (Image, 1998), 138.
3. David Scott, *Stuart Hall's Voice: Intimations of an Ethics of Receptive Generosity* (Duke University Press, 2017).
4. Scott, *Stuart Hall's Voice*, 127.

Select Bibliography

Agamben, Giorgio. *Remnants of Auschwitz: The Witness and the Archive*. Trans. Daniel Heller-Roazen. Zone Books, 2002.

Alexievich, Svetlana. *The Unwomanly Face of War*. Trans. Larissa Volokhonsky and Richard Pevear. Random House, 2018.

Bakhtin, Mikhail. *The Dialogic Imagination*. Trans. Caryl Emerson and Michael Holquist. University of Texas Press, 2008.

Bohm, David. *On Dialogue*. Taylor and Francis, 2004.

Buber, Martin. *The Way of Man According to the Teachings of Hasidism*. Wilcox & Follett, 1951.

Chandola, Tripta. *Listening into Others: An Ethnographic Exploration in Govindpuri*. Institute of Network Cultures, 2020.

Derrida, Jacques. "'A Self-Unsealing Poetic Text': Poetics and Politics of Witnessing." Trans. Rachel Bowlby. In *Revenge of the Aesthetic: The Place of Literature in Theory Today*, ed. Michael P. Clark, 180–207. University of California Press, 2010.

"Earwitness Inventory, 2018–Ongoing." Lawrence Abu Hamdan. Accessed February 27, 2026. http://lawrenceabuhamdan.com/earwitness-inventory.

El-Wardany, Haytham. *How to Disappear*. Trans. Jennifer Peterson and Robin Moger. Kayfa ta, 2013.

Felman, Shoshana, and Dori Laub. *Testimony: Crises of Witnessing in Literature, Psychoanalysis, and History*. Routledge, 1992.

Frankel, Estelle. *The Wisdom of Not-Knowing: Discovering a Life of Wonder by Embracing Uncertainty*. Shambhala Publications, 2017.

Fricker, Miranda. *Epistemic Injustice: Power and the Ethics of Knowing*. Oxford University Press, 2007.

Glassman, Bernie. *Bearing Witness: A Zen Master's Lessons in Making Peace*. Bell Tower, 1999.

Hagood, Mack. *Hush: Media and Sonic Self-Control*. Duke University Press, 2019.

Han, Byung-Chul. *Infocracy: Digitization and the Crisis of Democracy*. Trans. Daniel Steuer. Polity Press, 2022.

Kaminsky, Ilya. *Deaf Republic*. Graywolf Press, 2019.

Kimmerer, Robin Wall. *Braiding Sweetgrass: Indigenous Wisdom, Scientific Knowledge*. Milkweed Editions, 2013.

Levinas, Emmanuel. *Ethics and Infinity: Conversations with Philippe Nemo*. Trans. Richard A. Cohen. Duquesne University Press, 1985.

Lipari, Lisbeth. *Listening, Thinking, Being: Toward an Ethics of Attunement*. Pennsylvania State University Press, 2014.

Luiselli, Valeria. *Tell Me How It Ends: An Essay in Forty Questions*. 4th Estate, 2017.

"Machine Listening." Machine Listening. Accessed February 27, 2026. https://machinelistening.exposed/.

Milner, Marion. *A Life of One's Own*. Routledge, 2011.

Murphy, Kate. *You're Not Listening: What You're Missing and Why It Matters*. Celadon Books, 2019.

Oliveros, Pauline. *Quantum Listening*. Ignota Books, 2022.

Pomerantsev, Peter. *This Is Not Propaganda: Adventures in the War Against Reality*. Faber & Faber, 2019.

Rosa, Hartmut. *The Uncontrollability of the World*. Trans. James C. Wagner. Polity Press, 2020.

Schuppli, Susan. *Material Witness*. MIT Press, 2020.

Scott, David. *Stuart Hall's Voice: Intimations of an Ethics of Receptive Generosity*. Duke University Press, 2017.

Sontag, Susan. *Regarding the Pain of Others*. Farrar, Straus and Giroux, 2003.

Toop, David. *Sinister Resonance: The Mediumship of the Listener*. A&C Black, 2010.

Tsing, Anna Lowenhaupt. *The Mushroom at the End of the World*. Princeton University Press, 2015.

Turow, Joseph. *The Voice Catchers: How Marketers Listen In to Exploit Your Feelings, Your Privacy, and Your Wallet*. Yale University Press, 2021.

Vazquez Melken, Rolando. *Vistas of Modernity: Decolonial Aesthesis and the End of the Contemporary*. Mondrian Fund, 2020.

Weil, Simone. *Waiting for God*. Trans. Emma Craufurd. Harper Perennial, 1973.

Woolf, Virginia. *The Waves*. Vintage Classics, 2021.

Index

INDEX

INDEX

INDEX

INDEX

INDEX

INDEX